Every recipe in this book gives information on:

– the **number of servings**
– the **preparation time, including cooking time**
– the **nutritional value** per portion

The following symbols are used:

■   = simple
■ ■   = more complicated
■ ■ ■   = demanding

kcal   = kilocalories (1 kcal=4.184 kJ)
P   = protein
F   = fat
C   = carbohydrate

NB.   1 gram protein contains about 4 kcal
            1 gram fat contains about 9 kcal
            1 gram carbohydrate contains about 4 kcal

Throughout the book all weights and measures are given first in metric, then in imperial quantities. For example: 100g/4oz or 600ml/1 pint.

g   = gram
kg   = kilogram
ml   = millilitre
l   = litre
cm   = centimetre
oz   = ounce
fl oz   = fluid ounce
lb   = pound
in   = inch
tbsp   = tablespoon (about 15g)
tsp   = teaspoon (about 5g)
pinch   = about 1g

All temperatures are given in Celsius and Fahrenheit and refer to the settings used on conventional electric ovens. The corresponding gas mark is also given.

180°C/350°F = Gas Mark 4
200°C/400°F = Gas Mark 6
230°C/450°F = Gas Mark 8

– If you have a fan-assisted oven, the temperatures given should be reduced by 30°C/85°F.
– Times and settings for microwave ovens are only given in the section on microwave recipes.

EGG DISHES
BAKES & GRATINS

RECIPES AND PHOTOGRAPHY

AN INTRODUCTION TO EGGS

– Friedrich W. Ehlert –
– Odette Teubner, Kerstin Mosny –

HEARTY HOME COOKING

– Rotraud Degner –
– Pete Eising –

DISHES FROM AROUND THE WORLD

– Rotraud Degner –
– Ulrich Kerth –

COOKING FOR SPECIAL OCCASIONS

– Marianne Kaltenbach –
– Rolf Feuz –

WHOLEFOOD RECIPES

– Doris Katharina Hessler –
– Ansgar Pudenz –

QUICK-AND-EASY RECIPES

– Cornelia Adam –
– Michael Brauner –

MICROWAVE RECIPES

– Monika Kellermann –
– Odette Teubner, Kerstin Mosny –

LEAN CUISINE

– Monika Kellermann –
– Anschlag & Goldmann –

Translated by UPS Translations, London
Edited by Josephine Bacon and Ros Cocks

CLB 4208
Published originally under the title
"Das Neue Menu: Eierspeisen, Aufläufe und Gratins"
by Mosaik Verlag GmbH, Munich
© Mosaik Verlag, Munich
Project co-ordinator: Peter Schmoeckel
Editors: Ulla Jacobs, Cornelia Klaeger, Heidrun Schaaf, Dr Renate Zeltner
Layout: Peter Pleischl, Paul Wollweber

This edition published in 1995 by Grange Books
an imprint of Grange Books PLC,
The Grange, Grange Yard, London, SE1 3AG
English translation copyright © 1995 by CLB Publishing, Godalming, Surrey
Typeset by Image Setting, Brighton, E. Sussex
Printed and Bound in Singapore
All rights reserved
ISBN 1-85627-751-8

EGG DISHES
BAKES & GRATINS

Grange
BOOKS

Contents

An Introduction to Eggs

*N*o natural food has as much to offer as the egg! It contains nutritional elements vital to life and its versatility from the point of view of cooking methods is second to none. It can be transformed into delicious meals, ranging from stuffed, hard-boiled or poached eggs to juicy omelettes and light soufflés, with or without the addition of further ingredients.

By knowing the basic techniques for the preparation of egg dishes, and the important points about purchase and storage, a huge number of variants may be created. To make a real success of omelettes, stuffed or poached eggs and soufflés, this chapter takes you step by step through the essentials of the techniques.

TESTS FOR FRESHNESS

Use only fresh eggs; their flavour is best. The packing date gives one indication of freshness. The actual freshness can easily be determined with a few tests:

1. A freshly laid egg placed in cold water sinks straight to the bottom.

2. When an egg no older than one week is placed in water, its round end, where the air sac is located, will float slightly above the pointed end.

3. An egg which is more than two weeks old will stand almost vertically in the water. The buoyancy is provided by the expanded air sac.

Freshness can also be determined by observing a raw egg when it is cracked:

1a. The yolk of a fresh egg is plump, almost spherical. The white forms a cushion beneath it, but its outer edges will be more fluid.

2a. In an eight-day-old egg, the yolk is still well rounded. The white still forms a cushion, but its outer edges are more fluid than in the fresh egg.

3a. In an egg that is over two weeks old, the yolk is flat and the white is watery and runny.

STORAGE

Eggs are best stored with the small end down, leaving the rounded end, with its air sac upwards. They should not be stored with perishable or strong-smelling foods because there is a constant exchange of air, and therefore odour, through the porous shell. The exception is truffles, of course. Gourmets deliberately store these heavily-scented fungi with raw eggs so that the delicious smell will permeate the egg. Eggs can be stored for three to four weeks in a refrigerator. At room temperature the limit is one week. Raw egg yolks can be kept refrigerated for several days if covered with a little water.

Frozen out of their shells, eggs may be stored for up to four months. Frozen whites and yolks can also be stored separately. Before freezing, and depending on their intended use, yolks should be mixed with a pinch of either salt or sugar.

Store boiled eggs only in the refrigerator, as frozen boiled egg white turns waxy.

EQUIPMENT FOR PREPARATION OF EGG DISHES

For omelettes, special cast-iron omelette pans are most suitable. Their rims are slightly higher than those of normal pans, and are curved. For omelettes, scrambled or fried eggs, non-stick pans are also very good.

When baking use ovenproof ceramic or glass dishes.

For soufflés use special soufflé dishes with a high edge to take account of the rising soufflé, or smaller individual soufflé dishes.

In addition you will require utensils such as whisks, spatulas, a range of spoons, an egg piercer to prevent eggs cracking during boiling, and of course, egg cups and spoons. Where possible, boiled eggs should not come into contact with silver. Sulphur present in them causes dark spots of oxidation, which can also spoil an egg's delicate flavour. For this reason, always serve eggs in glass or porcelain. This also goes for other egg dishes.

When eating boiled eggs use plastic, stainless steel, mother-of-pearl or horn spoons.

A slotted spoon is an essential in egg cooking. This kitchen tool is an important assistant when poaching eggs and when deep-fat frying.

1.

2.

3.

1a.

2a.

3a.

SIMPLE EGG DISHES

An egg is the most versatile of foods. Whole, it may be boiled, baked, fried, poached or pickled. The white can be beaten until stiff and the yolk used as a binder. No matter what dish the egg is used for it must be fresh.

BOILING EGGS

Boiling times depend on the size of the egg. For an average egg to be cooked until just firm, an allowance of 5 minutes should be made for boiling. For hard-boiled eggs, about 10-12 minutes should be allowed.

The time is calculated from the instant that the water returns to the boil after the eggs are placed in it. For boiled eggs use only those with sound shells with no sign of cracks. Eggs that have come out of a refrigerator should first be warmed in warm water before being put in the boiling water. The temperature difference may otherwise cause the shells to break.

SEPARATING EGGS

For many egg dishes the eggs must be separated in order that the egg white may be beaten.

Crack the egg centrally on the sharp edge of a cup, and carefully break the shell in two.

Allow the yolk and the white to slip from one half of the shell to the other, and let the egg white spill into a dry, grease-free bowl ready for beating.

The egg yolk should be left without a trace of white adhering, and no yolk should be present in the white.

DEEP-FRYING EGGS

Deep-fried eggs are cooked out of their shells. Slip them into hot oil and fry them for 3-4 minutes at about 180°C/350°F. This is how to do it:

Heat the oil in a deep pan and slip in one egg.

1. With a pair of wooden spoons, immediately press the white around the yolk so that it is completely enclosed in white.

2. Remove the fried egg with a slotted spoon, place it on absorbent paper and drain thoroughly.

3. Fry the remaining eggs one by one. Season to taste with salt and pepper and serve.

1.

2.

POACHING EGGS

It is very important here to use fresh eggs which should be left in the refrigerator until the last possible moment before use. The white of an old egg will spread in the water and the result will not hold together.

Some vinegar is the only addition to the water; use about 2-3 tablespoons of vinegar to one litre of water. Salt should not be added as it affects the smooth surface of the white which is the desired result.

1. Bring the water and vinegar to the boil, then leave it simmering. Break the fresh, cold eggs individually into cups.

2. One by one slip the eggs into the water and, using a pair of spoons, smooth the white over the yolk of the egg until it is completely enclosed in white. Leave in the water for 3-4 minutes. Do not boil!

3. Remove the eggs with a slotted spoon and place them in lightly salted water.

4. Use a small kitchen knife to remove any filmy threads of white that remain on the surface.

5. For hot dishes, the poached eggs can be reheated in lightly salted water at a temperature of about 60°C/140°F. Drain them on a towel or kitchen paper.

The yolk of a poached egg should remain soft. By carefully applying finger pressure the condition of the yolk can be tested: around the yolk, the egg should yield slightly to the pressure.

1.

2.

3.

4.

5.

AN INTRODUCTION TO EGGS

STUFFING EGGS

1. Hard-boil the required number of eggs. Tap them gently on a work surface, and when the shells are cracked all over place the eggs in cold water.

2. Remove the shells carefully, so that none of the egg white comes away with them. Keep the peeled eggs in slightly salted water.

3. Cut a small sliver of white from either side of each egg to help them stand steady once they are cut in half.

4. Cut the eggs in half lengthways with a sharp knife and remove the yolks.

5. Rub the egg yolk through a fine sieve with some softened butter in the proportion three parts egg yolk to one part butter.

6. Season the mashed yolk with salt, mustard or paprika and beat it to a smooth cream.

7. Fit a piping bag with a large star tube and fill it with the yolk mixture. Pipe rosettes of the mixture into the halved whites.

3.

4.

5.

1.

2.

6.

7.

SCRAMBLED EGGS

To two eggs, add 3-4 tablespoons of cream, some salt and pepper and, if liked, 2 tablespoons of finely chopped bacon or a tablespoon of finely chopped chives or parsley. Use about 1 teaspoon of butter for cooking.

1. Break the eggs into a bowl.

2. Add the cream, salt and pepper and beat with a whisk until the egg white, yolk and cream are well mixed.

3. Add the bacon or herb and stir well.

4. Melt the butter in a heavy pan, if possible one reserved for eggs.

5. Pour the eggs gradually into the pan.

6. Stir with a wooden spoon as the mixture begins to thicken on the base of the pan.

7. While the scrambled eggs are still moist, fluffy and soft, turn them out onto warmed plates. Serve immediately.

3.

4.

5.

1.

2.

6.

7.

PREPARING OMELETTES

Omelettes are prepared with-out either flour or milk. They contain only fresh eggs. For one omelette allow 2-3 eggs, and some salt and pepper. Like scrambled eggs, omelettes can be prepared in a great variety of combina-tions with many ingredients. Special omelette or non-stick pans are ideal for cooking omelettes.

Fillings can be added direct to the egg mixture or rolled in the finished omelette.

1. Break the eggs into a bowl and season with salt and pep-per.

2. Beat the eggs well with a whisk without allowing them to become foamy.

3. Melt the butter and pour the eggs into the pan.

4. Stir the eggs with the back of a fork and keep the hot pan moving so that the eggs stiff-en evenly.

When stirring the soft egg towards the top of the omelette take care not to break the firmer layer on the base of the pan with the fork.

5. Tip the pan so that it stands at an angle and the omelette slides forward. Using the fork, fold up the omelette starting near the pan handle. Hold the pan at the very end of its handle and with your free hand, tap the handle smartly where it meets the pan itself. The omelette will slip all the way forwards and roll itself up.

1.

2.

3.

4.

5.

PREPARING PANCAKES

Pancakes are a classic dish that can make a satisfying meat-free meal if served with salad, or a tasty dessert if served with fruit purée, jam or lemon juice and sugar.

Herbs, mushrooms, seafood, bacon and ham can be mixed with the batter and cooked together; alternatively, pan-cakes can be made and kept ready for filling later. There are many ways to prepare the batter.

Some recipes call for whole eggs, while others use egg yolks with beaten egg white folded in afterwards. The egg white makes a particularly light and fluffy pancake.

For two pancakes measuring about 24 cm/10 inches across you will require: 60g/2oz plain flour, 150ml/ 5½ fl oz milk, 2 eggs, a pinch each of salt and sugar and two teaspoons of butter for frying.

1. Put the flour in a bowl. Add the milk, stirring all the time with a wire whisk, and mix until smooth.

2. Add the eggs, salt and sugar and beat vigorously.

3. For best results pass the batter through a fine sieve and leave to stand for about 30 minutes.

4. Heat some butter in a large frying pan, pour in half the batter and swirl it round. Let the batter stiffen, then remove the pan from the heat, flip the pancake and cook the other side.

5. Prepare the second pan-cake in the same way. Fill them to taste and serve.

1.

2.

3.

4.

5.

BAKES

There are several ways to make these. They may be based on a béchamel sauce, or on choux pastry, or on a mixture of meat and vegetables layered with potatoes, pasta or rice and covered in an egg and milk mixture.

PREPARING A CHEESE BAKE

Serves 2 or 4:

250ml/8 fl oz milk, 50g/2oz butter, salt, pepper, a little grated nutmeg, 75g/3oz flour, 4 eggs, separated, 125g/5oz grated cheese, butter and grated cheese for the dishes. Either four 9cm/3½-inch dishes or two 18cm/7-inch dishes.

1. Boil the milk with the butter, salt, pepper and nutmeg. Sift the flour onto greaseproof paper.

2. When the milk is boiling and the butter has melted, tip all the flour in at once.

3. Stir with a wooden spoon and keep heating and stirring until the mixture comes free from the pan and forms a ball.

4. Remove from the heat and gradually add the egg yolks.

5. Add the cheese and mix in well.

6. Beat the egg whites with a pinch of salt until standing in stiff peaks, then fold into the mixture.

7. Grease the dishes with butter, not forgetting their sides, and sprinkle them with cheese.

8. Spoon the mixture into the dishes.

9. Bake in a water bath in a preheated oven for 20–25 minutes at 220°C/425°F/ Gas Mark 7. Switch off the oven and leave the finished dishes to stand for 2-3 minutes before serving.

1.

2.

3.

4.

5.

6.

7.

8.

9.

Finished dish

POTATO AND PRAWN BAKE
(recipe page 120)

AU GRATIN DISHES

Here is another range of dishes that can be prepared in very different ways. Often they have much in common with the bakes described earlier. They can be presented with a sauce or quark and egg topping, or with cheese and breadcrumbs.

AUBERGINES AND TOMATOES AU GRATIN

A starter, side dish or vegetarian main course.

For 4 servings: 1 large aubergine, 4 tomatoes, pepper, 125ml/4 fl oz vegetable stock, 2 slices white bread, grated, 2 tablespoons grated cheese, 1 crushed garlic clove, 2 tbsps chopped fresh herbs, 30g/1oz butter for greasing and topping.

1. Wash the aubergines and tomatoes. Remove the tomato stalks. Cut aubergines and tomatoes into slices about 5 mm/¼ inch thick.

2. Butter an ovenproof dish. Arrange the tomato and aubergine slices in alternating and overlapping layers.

3. Sprinkle with pepper and pour in the stock.

4. Mix the breadcrumbs with the cheese, garlic and herbs and scatter over the dish. Dot with butter.

5. Heat the dish on the cooker, then bake in a preheated oven at 180°C/350°F/Gas Mark 4 for 30 minutes.

1.

2.

3.

4.

5.

MOULDS

These are more familiar as desserts, but can also be savoury main courses. Meat, fish, seafood, vegetables, bread and potatoes can all bring successful results. They often include a light batter, and eggs are an ever-present ingredient. These act as a binder to incorporate air and help the dish to rise.

POTATO MOULD

For 4 servings: 800g/1lb12oz peeled potatoes, 3 eggs, 150ml/4½ fl oz milk, salt, pepper, grated nutmeg, 1 tsp caraway seed, 2 tbsps finely chopped fresh marjoram, butter for greasing.

1. Cut the potatoes into slices about 5 mm/¼ inch thick. Boil for about 5 minutes in lightly salted water. Remove and drain on absorbent paper. Do not chill in cold water.

2. Beat the eggs and milk thoroughly and season with salt, pepper and nutmeg.

3. Cut a piece of greaseproof paper to line the bottom of an ovenproof dish. Spread butter over the dish and on the greaseproof paper.

4. Arrange circular layers of sliced potato in the dish. Sprinkle each layer with caraway seed and marjoram. Pour the beaten eggs over the potatoes. Place the dish in a water bath and bake in a preheated oven at 200°C/400°F/Gas Mark 6 for 45 minutes.

5. Turn out and remove the greaseproof paper.

1.

2.

3.

4.

5.

SOUFFLÉS

Because the volume of a soufflé expands by virtue of the beaten egg white when it is placed in the oven, the dish should be filled only two-thirds full, and it must be put in the bottom of the oven. During baking the oven door must on no account be opened, or the soufflé will instantly collapse! Carry the soufflé carefully to the table and serve immediately.

PREPARING A CHEESE SOUFFLÉ

For 4–6 servings:
60g/2oz butter, 60g/2oz plain flour, 500ml/16 fl oz milk, salt, pepper, nutmeg, 150g/5½oz Gruyère cheese, 6 eggs, butter and flour for the dish.

1. Butter the bottom of several small soufflé dishes or a single large dish and sprinkle with flour.

2. Melt the butter in a saucepan, add the flour and cook gently, stirring. Gradually add the milk, stirring constantly. Leave to cook thoroughly for one minute, then add seasonings.

3. Stir in the cheese and remove the pan from the heat. Heat the oven to 180°C/350°F/Gas Mark 4.

4. Separate the eggs. Blend the yolks, one by one, with the prepared sauce. Beat the egg whites until stiff and carefully fold them into the mixture.

5. Spoon the soufflé mixture into the dish. Run a knife around between the rim of the dish and the mixture to help the soufflé rise.

6. Place the dish in the bottom of the oven. Bake for 15 minutes, then raise the temperature to 200°C/400°F/Gas Mark 6 and bake for a further 30 minutes. Serve the risen soufflé immediately.

1.

2.

3.

4.

5.

6.

Soufflé

WHISKING EGG WHITES

To make really stiff egg whites, the whisk and bowl must be completely free of grease and perfectly dry. Adding sugar to the egg whites part way through whisking makes for a firmer result.

1. Put the separated egg whites in a clean, dry mixing bowl.

2. Using a balloon whisk or electric mixer, begin beating slowly, then increase to high speed.

3. The egg white is stiff when it stands in peaks and the surface appears dull.

1.

2.

3.

Hearty Home Cooking

*B*akes and gratins are a tried and tested feature of home cooking. They are equally popular as main courses, starters or snacks. Vegetables are high on the list of favourite ingredients for airy soufflés and savoury bakes, such as Spinach Soufflé and many others. However, cheese, meat, rice and mushrooms also give excellent results. Solid meals like Bread and Mushroom Bake or unusual dishes like Wholemeal Vegetable Goulash Pie should also put in the occasional appearance. Egg cuisine by no means begins and ends with fried eggs: think of more unusual dishes like Scrambled Eggs with Herbs and Cheese, Morels or Smoked Fish; Poached Eggs with Mustard Sauce; Omelette with Chicken Livers and Pancakes au Gratin with Meat Ragoût.

Baked Pancakes with Cheese Filling (recipe page 35)

SCRAMBLED EGGS WITH MORELS

SERVES 4 ■

Preparation and cooking time: 15 minutes
Soaking time: 1 hour
Kcal per portion: 370
P = 18g, F = 28g, C = 13g

100g/4oz fresh or 20g/3/4oz dried morels or other mushrooms
1 shallot
45g/1½oz butter
50g/2oz lean bacon
8 eggs
salt
freshly ground black pepper
freshly grated nutmeg
4 vol-au-vent cases or 4 slices of white toast
1 tsp chopped parsley

After washing thoroughly, cut large morels into halves or quarters.

1. Soak the dried mushrooms in cold water for 1 hour; place fresh ones in cold water for 5 minutes. Wash them thoroughly under running water, one at a time. Dry on absorbent paper. Cut large pieces into halves or quarters.

Add the morels to the fried bacon and shallot and fry gently for 5 minutes.

TIP

Morels must be washed very thoroughly because, fresh or dry, they are always slightly gritty.

Stir in diced butter.

2. Peel the shallot and dice very finely. Heat 30g/1oz of the butter in a non-stick pan and fry the shallot until it turns transparent.
3. Dice the bacon and add it to the diced shallot in the pan. Fry for a short time then add the mushrooms and fry gently for 5 minutes until all liquid has evaporated.
4. Beat the eggs, salt, pepper and nutmeg with a wire whisk until they begin to

foam slightly. Pour the beaten egg over the mushrooms and stir all the time until it reaches a creamy consistency. Add the rest of the butter in tiny pieces while stirring.
5. Serve the scrambled eggs in the vol-au-vent cases or on white toast. Sprinkle with parsley.
Side dish: watercress salad.

SCRAMBLED EGGS WITH HERBS AND CHEESE

SERVES 4 ■ ■

Preparation and cooking time: 15 minutes
Kcal per portion: 360
P = 20g, F = 25g, C = 15g

8 eggs
salt
freshly ground black pepper
40g/1½oz Cheddar cheese
2 tbsps finely chopped herbs (parsley, chives, chervil, 1–2 tarragon sprigs)
2 tsps English mustard
60g/2oz butter
2 tomatoes to garnish (optional)
4 slices of toasted wholemeal bread

1. Lightly beat the eggs, salt and pepper with a wire whisk until they begin to foam slightly. Grate the cheese and mix with the herbs and mustard until they form a paste.
2. Take two non-stick pans and melt 15g/½oz butter in each, then divide the eggs between them. Stir with a wooden spoon until the eggs begin to thicken. (The eggs can be cooked in one large pan, but it is less easy to get the desired creamy consistency in this way.) Gradually add the remaining butter.
3. Continue stirring the eggs until they have a creamy consistency. Blend the cheese paste with the scrambled eggs and pile onto the toast. Serve garnished with tomato wedges if desired.

BAKED EGGS

SERVES 4 ■

Preparation and cooking time: 30 minutes
Kcal per portion: 175
P = 15g, F = 13g, C = 1g

7 eggs
salt
1 bunch of chives, finely chopped
3 anchovy fillets
1 tsp capers
1 tbsp finely chopped fresh parsley
freshly ground black pepper
freshly grated nutmeg
butter for the dish

1. Butter a shallow oven-proof dish well. Heat the oven to 200°C/400°F/Gas Mark 6.
2. Break four of the eggs one at a time into the dish; sprinkle with salt and chives. Separate the three remaining eggs.

TIP

This dish looks even more appetising when prepared in small individual dishes. A little finely chopped bacon can be added to the egg mixture.

3. Drain and chop the anchovy fillets and mix them thoroughly with the egg yolks, capers and parsley. Season with pepper and nutmeg. Whisk the egg whites until stiff, fold them into the egg yolks and pour the mixture over the eggs in the dish.
4. Bake in the middle of the oven for about 15 minutes until golden yellow.
Side dish: rye bread rolls and a mixed salad.

TANGY BAKED EGGS

SERVES 4 ■
*Preparation and cooking
time: 40 minutes
Kcal per portion: 270
P = 18g, F = 18g, C = 8g*

*9 eggs, 6 hard-boiled
half a horseradish root or
1 bunch watercress
1 stale bread roll
15g/½oz butter
6 tbsps milk
salt
butter for the dish*

1. Butter a shallow dish generously. Heat the oven to 200°C/400°F/Gas Mark 6.
2. Cut the 6 hard-boiled eggs in half and place them in the dish with their cut sides facing down. Peel and grate the horseradish finely, or chop the watercress, and scatter it over the eggs.

Mix the diced bread roll with the egg and milk mixture.

3. Heat the butter in a small pan. Cut the roll into cubes and fry it in the butter until bright yellow.
4. Whisk the remaining eggs well with the milk and salt, then mix with the bread. Pour the mixture over the hard-boiled eggs in the dish. Place on the middle shelf of the oven for 20–25 minutes until the beaten egg is just firm.
Side dish: chicory salad with watercress and crusty bread.

BISMARCK EGGS

SERVES 4 ■
*Preparation and cooking
time: 15 minutes
Kcal per portion: 165
P = 14g, F = 12g, C = 0g*

*100g/4oz cooked ham
4 eggs
salt
freshly ground black pepper
4 tbsps freshly grated
Parmesan cheese
butter for the dish
4 lettuce leaves*

1. Cut the ham into thin strips. Butter four ovenproof dishes with lids; alternatively, use four cups and cover them with kitchen foil.
2. Break an egg into each dish and season with salt and pepper. Mix the cheese and ham together and sprinkle over the eggs.
3. Cover the dishes or cups with their lids or foil. Boil some water in a shallow pan and places the dishes in the water. The top third of each dish should stand above the level of the water. Simmer the eggs for 10 minutes, until just set.

> **TIP**
>
> *For a main
> course, double
> the quantities
> and serve with
> spinach or
> mashed potatoes.*

4. Arrange the lettuce leaves on four small plates. Turn one egg out onto each leaf. Serve as a starter before a light main course.
Side dish: buttered toast and mixed salad with chives.

Break an egg into each dish and season with salt and pepper.

Sprinkle the mixture of ham and Parmesan cheese over the eggs.

Cover the dishes with foil and place them in a pan with hot water.

SCRAMBLED EGGS WITH SMOKED FISH

SERVES 4 ■
*Preparation and cooking
time: 15 minutes
Kcal per portion: 565
P = 40g, F = 45g, C = 1g*

*2 bloaters or smoked
mackerel fillets
60g/2oz butter
8 eggs
4 tbsps water or milk
freshly ground black pepper
3–4 fresh dill sprigs*

1. Carefully skin the smoked fish and remove all the bones. Break the flesh into pieces.
2. Heat the butter in a large frying pan and fry the fish for a short time.
3. Beat together the eggs, water or milk, salt, pepper and one teaspoon of

Carefully skin the smoked fish and remove the bones, before frying.

chopped dill until the mixture foams slightly. Pour it over the fish. Stir and break up the eggs with a fork. Remove the pan from the heat as soon as the egg begins to set. Garnish with dill sprigs and serve immediately, as it is or on white bread fried in butter.
Side dish: potatoes boiled in their jackets and cucumber salad.

OMELETTE WITH CHICKEN LIVERS

SERVES 4 ■ ■
*Preparation and cooking
    time: 25 minutes
Kcal per portion: 390
P = 21g, F = 31g, C = 2g*

*8 eggs
salt
freshly ground black pepper
4 tarragon sprigs
6 chicken livers
90g/3½ oz butter
2 shallots
100ml/4 fl oz red wine
4 tbsps crème fraîche*

*Quickly fry the livers on all sides
in melted butter.*

1. Using a fork, beat the eggs, salt and pepper until the yolks and whites are completely mixed together. Chop the tarragon sprigs very finely and add them to the egg mixture.
2. Remove any fat or gristle from the livers and cut each one into six pieces.
3. Heat 15g/½oz of the butter in a small pan and quickly fry the livers all over, leaving them slightly pink on the inside. Season with salt and pepper. Remove them from the pan and keep warm.

*Cook the omelettes one after the
other in a non-stick pan.*

> **TIP**
>
> *These omelettes
> make a starter
> for four or a
> satisfying main
> dish for two.*

4. Peel the shallots and chop finely. Heat 30g/1oz of butter in the pan, add the shallots and fry until transparent. Add the red wine and reduce by half. Add the crème fraîche and continue cooking until the sauce has a creamy consistency.
5. Heat the remaining butter in a second small pan and make four omelettes. Do not fold them in the usual way

*Mix the livers with the red wine
sauce and spread it over the
omelettes.*

but lay flat on heated plates and keep warm. Heat the livers for a short time in the red wine sauce. Spoon some of the filling onto the middle of each omelette and fold in half.
Side dish: lamb's lettuce, radicchio and tomato salad.

POACHED EGGS WITH MUSTARD SAUCE

SERVES 4 ■
*Preparation and cooking
    time: 20 minutes
Kcal per portion: 495
P = 16g, F = 47g, C = 1g*

*salt
1 tbsp vinegar
8 eggs*

MUSTARD SAUCE:
*150g/5½oz butter
2 tbsps water
2 egg yolks
juice of ½ lemon
freshly ground white pepper
1 tbsp English mustard
a few tarragon leaves to
    garnish*

*Slip the eggs into the water with a
ladle.*

1. To poach the eggs put 1l/1¾ pints of water into a large shallow pan with some salt and the vinegar. Bring to the boil, then break the eggs one by one into a ladle and carefully slip them into the water so that the white fully encloses the yolk. Simmer very gently for 3 minutes, then remove the eggs from the water with a slotted spoon and keep them warm in a bowl containing some hot water.

*Whisk the egg yolks into the
butter-water mixture with a wire
whisk.*

> **TIP**
>
> *Do not cook the
> mustard, but add
> it to the sauce
> just as cooking is
> completed.*

2. To make the mustard sauce, finely dice the butter. Melt 15g/½oz of it in a heavy pan, add the water and mix thoroughly with a wire whisk. Remove the pan from the heat and add the egg yolks, stirring all the time. Return the pan to the heat and gradually add the

*Over a low heat, add butter to the
egg yolks.*

remaining butter, one piece at a time; whisk constantly and do not allow to boil.
3. Add the lemon juice and season the sauce with a little salt and pepper. Remove it from the heat and whisk in the mustard.
4. Arrange two poached eggs on each plate and pour over the mustard sauce. Serve at once garnished with tarragon.
Side dish: new potatoes.
Recommended wine: a fruity German white.

PANCAKES AU GRATIN WITH MEAT RAGOÛT

PANCAKES AU GRATIN WITH MEAT RAGOÛT

SERVES 4 ▪▪

Preparation and cooking
time: 1 hour
Kcal per portion: 570
P = 26g, F = 40g, C = 26g

FOR THE PANCAKES:
8 tbsps flour
½ tsp salt
4 eggs
500ml/16 fl oz milk
butter for frying and greasing

FOR THE FILLING:
1 small onion
3 tbsps oil
150g/5½oz minced steak
50g/2oz minced pork
½ tsp paprika
small piece of fresh ginger
*   root, finely chopped*
20g/¾oz dried mushrooms,
*   soaked*
2 tbsps tomato purée
20g/¾oz flour
125ml/4 fl oz single cream
salt
freshly grated Parmesan
*   cheese to serve*

1. To make the pancakes, mix the flour and salt in a bowl. Add the eggs and milk, stirring all the time.
2. In a medium frying pan, heat a little butter and cook eight pancakes.

Add the cream, flour and tomato purée mixture to the meat and mushrooms.

Spread the ragoût over the pancakes and roll them up.

Place the rolled pancakes on a buttered dish and sprinkle with grated Parmesan.

TIP

For a light evening meal, fill half the pancakes with ragoût and the other half with asparagus or peas.

3. To make the filling, finely chop the onion. Heat the oil in a pan and fry the onion. Add the meats with the paprika, ginger root and mushrooms and brown thoroughly. Mix the flour with the tomato purée and cream, stir into the mixture and cook for 5 minutes. Season with salt to taste.
4. Heat the oven to 220°C/425°F/Gas Mark 7. Butter an ovenproof dish.
5. Spread the ragoût over the pancakes and roll them up. Pack into the dish, sprinkle with Parmesan cheese and brown for 10 minutes in the top of the oven.
Side dish: celery salad.

BAKED PANCAKES WITH CHEESE FILLING

(photo page 26/27)

SERVES 4 ▪

Preparation and cooking
time: 1 hour
Kcal per portion: 640
P = 34g, F = 46g, C = 23g

FOR THE PANCAKES:
60g/2oz flour
125ml/4 fl oz milk
salt
4 eggs
30g/1oz butter

FOR THE SAUCE:
30g/1oz butter
30g/1oz flour
250ml/8 fl oz milk
salt
frshly ground black pepper
freshly grated nutmeg

FOR THE FILLING:
100g/4oz cooked ham
100g/4oz Mozzarella cheese
150g/5½oz Ricotta cheese
50g/2oz grated Parmesan
*   cheese*

extra butter for frying,
*   greasing and browning*
30g/1oz grated Parmesan for
*   browning*

1. Put the flour in a bowl and add the milk, salt and eggs, stirring all the time. Melt the butter and add it to the batter last of all.
2. In a medium frying pan, heat a little butter and cook paper-thin pancakes, setting each aside to cool.
3. Make the sauce by melting the butter in a pan, adding the flour and cooking gently until bright yellow. Stir with a wire whisk and while doing so, gradually add the milk; cook for 5 minutes. Season the sauce with salt, pepper and nutmeg to taste.
4. Dice the ham and Mozzarella very finely. Rub the Ricotta through a sieve and blend it with the sauce. Add the ham, Mozzarella

Mix diced ham and Mozzarella into the sauce with the grated Parmesan.

Spread 1-2 tablespoons of stuffing over each pancake and roll them up.

and grated Parmesan. Season with salt and pepper.
5. Heat the oven to 220°C/425°F/Gas Mark 7.
6. Spread some of the stuffing on each pancake and roll them up. Butter a shallow dish and arrange the pancakes in it. Sprinkle with grated Parmesan and dot with butter. Place on the top shelf of the oven until the cheese has melted and browned.
These very delicate pancakes are also excellent served as a dessert with a sweet filling.
Side dish: thick tomato sauce or a tomato salad.

CHEESE SOUFFLÉ

SERVES 4 ■
*Preparation and cooking
    time: 1 hour
Kcal per portion: 535
P = 27g, F = 39g, C = 19g*

*60g/2oz butter
60g/2oz flour
500ml/16 fl oz milk
salt
freshly ground black pepper
freshly grated nutmeg
150g/5½oz Gruyère cheese,
    grated
6 eggs, separated
extra butter and dry
    breadcrumbs for the dish*

1. Butter a single 2l/3½-pint soufflé dish or four small dishes and sprinkle with breadcrumbs.
2. Melt the butter, add the flour and cook gently until it turns bright yellow. Stir with a wire whisk and while doing so, gradually add the milk; cook for 1 minute. Season with salt, pepper and nutmeg to taste.
3. Stir in the cheese and remove the pan from the heat.
4. Heat the oven to 180°C/350°F/Gas Mark 4.
5. One by one, stir the egg yolks into the cheese sauce. Whisk the egg whites until stiff and carefully fold them into the mixture.
6. Spoon the soufflé mix into the dish; fill it no more than two-thirds full. Run a knife round inside the dish to help the soufflé rise.
7. Place the dish in the middle of the oven. Bake for 15 minutes, then raise the temperature to 200°C/400°F/Gas Mark 6 and bake the soufflé for a further 30 minutes. Serve immediately to prevent the soufflé collapsing.
Side dish: frisée lettuce with walnuts.

CHICKEN SOUFFLÉ

(photo page 25)

SERVES 4 ■
*Preparation and cooking
    time: 1 hour
Kcal per portion: 335
P = 24g, F = 23g, C = 8g*

*250g/8oz cooked chicken,
    skin removed
50g/2oz bacon
40g/1¼oz butter
40g/1¼oz flour
250ml/9 fl oz chicken stock
2 tbsps single cream
4 eggs, separated
salt
freshly ground white pepper
a few tarragon leaves
1 tsp grated lemon rind
butter for the dish*

1. Butter a 2l/3½-pint soufflé dish. Heat the oven to 200°C/400°F/Gas Mark 6.
2. Finely mince the meat and bacon in a food processor.
3. Melt the butter in a heavy pan, add the flour and cook gently until it turns bright yellow, then add the chicken stock, stirring all the time. Cook for 5 minutes. Add the cream, remove the pan from the heat and stir in the egg yolks one at a time. Season well with salt and pepper.
4. Chop the tarragon leaves. Mix together the tarragon, lemon rind, meat and sauce. Whisk the egg whites until stiff and fold into the soufflé mixture.
5. Fill the soufflé dish two-thirds full and bake in the middle of the oven for about 25 minutes. Serve immediately to prevent the soufflé collapsing. This soufflé is also excellent if spiced with curry powder, in which case the tarragon should be omitted.
Side dish: sweet peppers, salad or mango chutney.

Finely mince the meat and bacon in a food processor.

Beat the sauce with a wire whisk and add the egg yolks.

Fold the stiffly beaten egg whites into the soufflé mixture.

BUCKWHEAT PANCAKES WITH BACON

SERVES 4 ■
*Preparation and cooking
    time: 40 minutes
Standing time: 4 hours
Kcal per portion: 245
P = 13g, F = 6g, C = 35g*

*150g/5½oz buckwheat flour
½ tsp salt
500ml/16 fl oz buttermilk
100g/4oz bacon
cranberry sauce to serve*

1. Mix the buckwheat flour with the salt in a bowl. Beat together the buttermilk and the eggs and gradually whisk this mixture into the flour until a smooth batter results. Leave to stand for a few hours.

> **TIP**
>
> *Cranberry compote makes a good substitute for syrup.*

2. Dry-fry a few slices of the bacon in a small pan until crisp. Pour some of the batter over the bacon, fry until light brown, turn carefully and fry on the other side. Set aside on a plate and keep warm by covering with another plate and standing over a pan of boiling water.
3. Continue making pancakes until the bacon and batter are all used up.
4. The sauce can be spread over the pancakes when they are served at the table.
Side dish: lettuce or frisée.
Recommended drinks: buttermilk or beer.

CABBAGE MOULD

SERVES 4 ■ ■
*Preparation and cooking
    time: 1 hour 30 minutes
Kcal per portion: 320
P = 22g, F = 20g, C = 13g*

*1 white cabbage, about 1kg/
    2¼lbs
salt
15g/½oz butter
1 tsp caraway seeds
200g/7oz lamb
100g/4oz bacon
1 stale bread roll
125ml/4 fl oz milk
1 piece fresh ginger root or ½
    tsp powdered ginger
2 eggs
grated rind of ½ lemon
½ tsp English mustard
freshly ground black pepper
butter for the dish*

1. Butter a 2l/3½-pint pudding basin with lid.
2. Cut out the stem of the
cabbage. Bring a generous
amount of salted water to
the boil, and boil the cabbage until its outer leaves are
just turning soft. Remove a
few leaves to line the basin
and set them aside on
absorbent paper. Chop the
remaining leaves very finely.
3. Heat the butter in a large
pan, then fry the caraway
seeds and finally the
chopped cabbage.
4. Coarsely chop the lamb
and bacon, then mince very
finely in a food processor.
Soak the bread roll in the
milk and chop the ginger
finely.
5. Mix the cabbage with the
meat, the squeezed-out roll,
the eggs, ginger root, lemon
rind and mustard. Season
well with salt and pepper.
6. Line the pudding basin
with cabbage leaves and fill
with the mixture. Cover with
a few more cabbage leaves
and fit the lid to the bowl.
7. Place the bowl on an
upturned plate in a pan of
water. The water should

*Having removed the outer leaves,
chop the remaining cabbage finely.*

*Line the pudding basin with cab-
bage leaves, and then fill with the
chopped cabbage and meat.*

reach halfway up the bowl.
Close the pan with a lid and
cover it with a damp cloth so
that the pudding heats evenly throughout.
8. Cook the pudding for 1
hour then remove it from the
water and leave it to stand
for 10 minutes. Turn it out
onto a heated plate and cut
into portions with a sharp
knife.
A late Savoy cabbage makes
a good substitute for white
cabbage. The young Savoy is
not so good as its leaves tear
easily.
Side dish: caper sauce and
mashed potatoes.

SPINACH SOUFFLÉ

SERVES 4 ■
*Preparation and cooking
    time: 1 hour
Kcal per portion: 465
P = 23g, F = 36g, C = 12g*

*200g/7oz spinach, blanched
90g/3½oz butter
3 shallots
75g/3oz cooked ham
salt
freshly ground white pepper
freshly grated nutmeg
40g/1¼oz flour
250ml/8 fl oz milk
5 eggs, separated
75g grated Parmesan cheese
butter for the dish*

1. Butter a 2l/3½-pint soufflé
dish.
2. Drain the spinach well
and chop it finely in a food
processor; do not purée.
3. Melt 30g/1oz butter in a
small pan. Peel the shallots,
chop them finely and fry in
the butter until transparent.
Chop the ham very finely
and add it to the pan with
the spinach. Cook gently for
5 minutes, then season with
salt, pepper and nutmeg.
4. Melt the remaining butter
in another pan and add the
flour. Cook gently until the
flour turns bright yellow,
then add the milk, stirring all
the time. Bring to the boil
once, then remove the pan
from the heat and stir in the
egg yolks, one by one. Blend
the spinach mixture and
cheese with the sauce.
5. Heat the oven to
180°C/350°F/Gas Mark 4.
6. Whisk the egg whites until
they stand in stiff peaks and
carefully fold into the soufflé
mixture. Fill the dish two-
thirds full.
7. Bake the soufflé in the
middle of the oven for 15
minutes, then raise the temperature to 200°C/400°F/
Gas Mark 6 and bake for a
further 30 minutes. Serve
immediately.

CAULIFLOWER SOUFFLÉ

SERVES 4 ■ ■
*Preparation and cooking
    time: 1 hour
Kcal per portion: 315
P = 20g, F = 24g, C = 5*

*1 cauliflower, about 500g/1lb
    2oz
salt
50g/2oz butter
freshly ground white pepper
freshly grated nutmeg
1 tsp hot curry powder
80g/3oz Gruyère cheese,
    grated
4 egg yolks
8 egg whites
butter and flour for the dish*

1. Cook the cauliflower in
lightly salted boiling water
for 15 minutes. Break it into
florets and dry on absorbent
paper. Purée in a food
processor.
2. Dice the butter finely. Put
the purée in a pan and heat
it, adding the butter piece by
piece. Season with pepper,
nutmeg and curry powder,
then stir in the cheese. Leave
to cool.
3. Heat the oven to
200°C/400°F/Gas Mark 6.
4. Add the egg yolks to the
purée one by one. Whisk the
egg whites until stiff. Stir
about one-fifth into the
purée, then carefully fold in
the remainder.
5. Butter four small soufflé
dishes and sprinkle them
with flour. Fill with soufflé
mixture to a depth of no
more than two-thirds. Run a
knife around between the
mixture and the side of the
dish to help the soufflé rise.
6. Bake in the middle of the
oven for about 18 minutes,
until well risen and golden.
Serve immediately.
Side dish: pickles and
French bread.

CARROT AND POTATO BAKE

SERVES 4 ■■
*Preparation and cooking
    time: 1 hour 30 minutes
Kcal per portion: 605
P = 30g, F = 38g, C = 35g*

*500g/1lb 2oz carrots
50g/2oz stale bread
250ml/8 fl oz milk
1 large onion
salt
300g/10oz potatoes
45g/1½oz butter
a few rosemary sprigs,
    chopped
1 tsp ground ginger
1 tsp sugar
200g/7oz Cheddar cheese,
    grated
4 eggs, separated
50g/2oz chopped almonds
2 tbsps chopped fresh parsley
freshly ground white pepper
50g/2oz breadcrumbs
butter for greasing and
    topping*

*Sprinkle the onions and carrots
with rosemary, ginger and sugar,
then braise very gently.*

*Put the potatoes through a potato
ricer while still hot.*

1. Butter a large soufflé dish
generously.
2. Scrub or scrape the carrots and cut them into thick
rings. Cut the bread into
small cubes and soften it in
the milk. Dice the onion.
Peel the potatoes and cook
them in salted water.
3. Melt 15g/½oz of the butter in a heavy pan and fry the
diced onion until it turns
transparent. Add the carrots,
sprinkle with rosemary, ginger and sugar and braise
until they just begin to
colour. Add 6 tablespoons of
water, cover the pan and
cook the carrots gently until
they are soft. Finally, purée
them in a blender or food
processor.
4. Heat the oven to
220°C/425°F/Gas Mark 7.
5. Drain the boiled potatoes
and put them through a
potato ricer, vegetable mill
or sieve while still hot. Melt
the remaining butter and
squeeze out the bread. Mix
these ingredients with the
carrots, the milk used to

soak the bread, 150g/5½oz
of the cheese, the whisked
egg yolks, the almonds and
parsley. Season well with salt
and pepper.
6. Whisk the egg whites until
stiff and fold them into the
potato mixture, then fill the
soufflé dish. Mix the remaining cheese with the breadcrumbs, scatter them over
the soufflé and dot the top
with butter. Cover the dish
with aluminium foil and bake
for 45 minutes in the middle
of the oven.
Serve as an accompaniment
to meat balls, chops or
sausages, or as a main
course with a salad.

VEGETABLES AU GRATIN

SERVES 4 ■■
*Preparation and cooking
    time: 1 hour
Kcal per portion: 810
P = 25g, F = 48g, C = 69g*

*250g/8oz long-grain rice
salt
4 tbsps pine nuts or cashew
    nuts
30g/1oz butter
500g/1lb 2oz broccoli
2 tbsps oil
20 button onions
250g/8oz carrots
250g/8oz mushrooms
freshly ground white pepper
2 tbsps chopped mixed fresh
    herbs (parsley, chives,
    chervil, dill)*

FOR THE MORNAY SAUCE:
*60g/2oz butter
45g/1½oz flour
250ml/9 fl oz milk
250ml/9 fl oz vegetable water
salt
freshly ground white pepper
freshly grated nutmeg
5 tbsps single cream
100g/4oz Cheddar cheese,
    grated
3 egg yolks
butter for the dish and as
    topping*

1. Butter a large soufflé dish.
2. Boil the rice in plenty of
salted water for 10–12 minutes or until just tender.
Drain well in a colander.
3. Fry the nuts in 1 tablespoon of the butter until yellow. Mix them with the rice.
Spread the rice and nuts
over the bottom of the soufflé dish.
4. Divide the broccoli into
florets and blanch for 8 minutes in boiling salted water.
Drain in a colander.
5. Heat the remaining butter
with the oil in a deep pan.
Peel the onions, add to the
pan and fry, tossing fre-
quently, until they turn a light
yellow. Scrub or scrape the
carrots, cut them into thin
rings and add the onions. Fry

*Beat the sauce thoroughly; no
lumps of flour should remain.*

gently for a further 10 minutes. Wipe and slice the
mushrooms; add to the vegetables in the pan and fry
gently for another 3 minutes.
Season with salt and pepper.
6. Mix the broccoli and
herbs with the vegetables in
the pan and spread them
over the bed of rice in the
dish.
7. Heat the oven to
220°C/425°F/Gas Mark 7.
8. To make the mornay
sauce, first melt the butter in
a heavy pan, then add the
flour and cook gently until it
turns a light yellow. Stir with
a wire whisk, and while
doing so, add the milk and
vegetable water (alternatively use 500ml/16 fl oz of milk
only). Simmer the sauce for
10 minutes, then season
with salt, pepper and nutmeg. Add the cream and
cheese. Remove the pan
from the heat and thicken
the sauce with the egg yolks.
Pour the sauce over the vegetables and dot with butter.
9. Bake for 15–20 minutes in
the top of the oven until
golden.
Side dish: cooked or raw
ham.

RICE SOUFFLÉ WITH MUSHROOMS

SERVES 4 ■■
*Preparation and cooking
    time: 1 hour
Kcal per portion: 395
P = 21g, F = 20g, C = 32g*

*150g/5½oz long-grain rice
salt
1 shallot
15g/½oz butter
150g/5½oz oyster mushrooms
    or chanterelles
2 tbsps sunflower seeds
50g/2oz smoked bacon
75g/3oz Emmental cheese,
    grated
5 eggs, separated
freshly ground white pepper
1 tbsp coarsely chopped herbs
    (parsley, chervil or dill)
butter and flour for the dish*

1. Grease a soufflé dish with butter and dust with flour.
2. Boil the rice in plenty of salted water for 12–15 minutes until soft but still nutty. Drain well in a colander.
3. Chop the peeled shallot finely and fry gently in the butter. Clean the mushrooms and cut up if necessary, add to the shallots and cook until soft.
4. Dry-fry the sunflower seeds in a small pan until they begin to darken. Chop the bacon very fine.
5. Heat the oven to 200°C/400°F/Gas Mark 6.
6. Mix together the rice, mushrooms, sunflower seeds, bacon and cheese in a bowl. Beat the egg yolks thoroughly with some salt and pepper and add them to the rice. Whisk the egg whites until they form stiff peaks. Stir a quarter of the whisked whites into the rice mixture, then carefully fold in the remainder.
7. Spoon the rice mixture into the soufflé dish. Run a knife round the inside of the dish to help the soufflé rise.

Gently fry the mushrooms with the finely chopped shallot until soft.

Lightly brown the sunflower seeds in a dry pan.

Stir beaten egg yolks into the mixture of rice, cheese, bacon, mushrooms and sunflower seeds.

8. Bake on the middle shelf of the oven for about 30 minutes until golden. Sprinkle with herbs and serve immediately.
Side dish: avocado and tomato salad.

ASPARAGUS AND RICE AU GRATIN

SERVES 4 ■
*Preparation and cooking
    time: 1 hour
Kcal per portion: 760
P = 28g, F = 45g, C = 64g*

*60g/2oz butter
1 small onion
300g/10oz risotto or short-
    grain rice
1l/1¾ pints hot beef stock
150g/5½oz cooked ham
500g/1lb2oz cooked
    asparagus tips (fresh or
    canned)
250ml/9 fl oz single cream
4 eggs
4 tbsps grated Parmesan
    cheese
salt
freshly ground black pepper
freshly grated nutmeg
butter for the dish*

1. Butter a large soufflé dish.
2. Heat 30g/1oz of the butter in a pan and fry the diced onion until transparent. Add the rice and fry for a few minutes until translucent, stirring constantly. Very gradually top up with boiling stock; the rice should simmer all the while, and be cooked by the time it has absorbed all the liquid; in about 20 minutes.
3. Heat the oven to 220°C/425°F/Gas Mark 7.
4. Cut the bacon into strips and toss with the asparagus in the remaining butter.
5. Beat the cream thoroughly with the eggs, Parmesan, salt, pepper and nutmeg.
6. When the rice is just tender remove the risotto from the heat and transfer it to the soufflé dish. Cover it with the asparagus and bacon mixture and pour the cream sauce over the top. Bake for 10–15 minutes in the middle of the oven until golden.

BREAD AND MUSHROOM BAKE

SERVES 4–6 ■■
*Preparation and cooking
    time: 1 hour
Kcal per portion (4 persons):
    480
P = 22g, F = 30g, C = 30g*

*5 stale rolls
375ml/15 fl oz hot milk
500g/1lb 2oz chanterelle or
    button mushrooms
1 onion
50g/2oz smoked streaky
    bacon
30g/1oz butter
1 tbsp chopped chervil
salt
frshly ground white pepper
3 eggs, separated
freshly grated nutmeg
100g/4oz Emmental cheese
butter for greasing and
    topping*

1. Butter a large soufflé dish.
2. Cut the rolls into thin slices, cover them with the hot milk and leave to soak. Wash and dry the mushrooms or wipe with a clean damp cloth. Dice the onion and bacon.
3. Heat half the butter in a medium pan. Fry the onion and bacon, then add the mushrooms and fry gently for about 10 minutes. Mix with the chervil and season.
4. Gently squeeze the milk out of the bread slices. Fry them in the remaining butter, then set aside. Beat the egg yolks with the milk, season with salt and nutmeg and mix with the bread.
5. Heat the oven to 200°C/400°F/Gas Mark 6.
6. Grate the cheese coarsely, then stir into the bread mixture along with the mushrooms. Whisk the egg whites until stiff, then fold into the mixture. Fill the soufflé dish, dot with butter and bake for 30–40 minutes until golden. Serve with tomato sauce.

WHOLEMEAL VEGETABLE
GOULASH PIE

WHOLEMEAL VEGETABLE GOULASH PIE

SERVES 4 ■■
*Preparation and cooking
time: 2 hours
Kcal per portion: 835
P = 24g, F = 63g, C = 45g*

FOR THE PASTRY:
*200g/7oz wholemeal flour
½ tsp baking powder
salt
150g/5½oz chilled butter
4 tbsps water*

FOR THE FILLING:
*200g/7oz beef steak
12 button onions
250g/8oz tomatoes
2 tbsps oil
salt
1 tbsp paprika
500ml/16 fl oz beef stock
250ml/9 fl oz single cream
1 tbsp flour
250g/8oz carrots
250g/8oz green beans or
    asparagus
150g/5½oz fresh or frozen
    peas*

*1 egg yolk
butter for greasing*

1. Grease a soufflé dish or large earthenware pie dish.
2. Begin making the pastry by thoroughly mixing the flour and baking powder in a bowl. Add the salt. Coarsely grate the cold butter into the flour and rub in well with the fingertips. Add the water and knead to a smooth dough. Cover with cling film and leave in the refrigerator for 30 minutes.
3. Cut the meat into cubes. Blanch and peel the tomatoes, remove the seeds and chop the flesh roughly. Heat the oil in a heavy pan and brown the meat lightly. Peel the onions, add to the pan with the tomatoes and cook gently for 10 minutes. Add the salt, paprika and stock and cook for 45 minutes or until the meat is tender.
4. Mix the cream with the

Cover the edge of the crust with a strip of pastry and press down firmly all around.

flour and stir into the meat sauce.
5. Clean and chop the carrots and beans or asparagus, boil them briefly in salted water with the peas and drain well. Mix with the meat.
6. Heat the oven to 200°C/400°F/Gas Mark 6.
7. Roll out the pastry. Cut out a top the size of the dish and also a long strip. Use a cutter to make small hearts or stars out of the scraps. Fill the dish with the meat and vegetables and cover with the pastry. Cut a cross in the centre of the top and dampen the edge. Press the strip of pastry around the edge of the dish so that it seals the top in place. Decorate with the pastry shapes and brush with beaten egg yolk.
8. Bake for 1 hour in the middle of the oven. Cut the pie at the table.
Instead of wholemeal shortcrust pastry, a 300g/10oz pack of frozen puff pastry (defrosted) can be used for this recipe.
Side dish: a mixed green salad.
Recommended drink: beer or red vin du pays.

BAKED PASTA

SERVES 4 ■■
*Preparation and cooking
    time: 1 hour 30 minutes
Kcal per portion: 845
P = 42g, F = 40g, C = 79g*

*400g/14oz macaroni
40g/1¼oz salt
4 litres/7 pints water*

FOR THE FILLING:
*250g/8oz chanterelles
1 small onion
15g/½oz butter
2 tbsps chopped parsley
250g/8oz cooked ham in a
    single piece
salt
freshly ground black pepper*

FOR THE SAUCE:
*250ml/8 fl oz milk
125ml/4 fl oz single cream
3 eggs
salt
100g/4oz Emmental or
    Gruyère cheese, grated*

*4 tbsps breadcrumbs
butter for greasing and
    topping*

1. Butter a shallow rectangular ovenproof dish or large cake tin.
2. In a large saucepan, bring the salted water to the boil, then add the unbroken macaroni. Cook for 12–15 minutes, according to the packet instructions, until the pasta is just al dente. Leave to drain well.
3. Meanwhile make the filling. Clean the mushrooms and dice the onions. Heat the butter in a pan and fry the onions until they turn transparent, then add the mushrooms. Fry gently for 5 minutes. Cut the ham into thin strips and mix with the mushrooms. Season with salt and pepper.
4. Make the sauce by beating together the milk, cream, eggs and salt, and finally adding the cheese.
5. Heat the oven to 200°C/400°F/Gas Mark 6.
6. Place a thin layer of mac-

Spread half the mushroom and gammon mixture evenly over the macaroni.

Pour sauce over every other layer of macaroni.

aroni lengthways in the dish. Cover with half the mushroom and ham mixture, then place another layer of macaroni over the top. Cover this with half the sauce, followed by another layer of macaroni and the rest of the mushroom and ham. Finally, cover with the remaining macaroni and top with the last of the sauce.
7. Sprinkle the top with breadcrumbs and dot with butter.
8. Bake in the middle of the oven for 40–45 minutes until golden brown. Serve cut in thick slices.
Side dishes: tomato sauce and green salad.
Recommended wine: red vin du pays.

*O*n a trip through the world of egg dishes, bakes and gratins, travellers discover new and interesting dishes from many lands. Take, for example, the difference between traditional British fried eggs and their Italian counterparts, which are always accompanied by garlic and tomatoes. Middle and Far Eastern ways with eggs are soon revealed by Chinese Pan-fried Eggs or Indian-style Scrambled Eggs.

Under the heading of international delicacies, the numerous omelettes of the French repertoire and Spanish tortilla variants are in a class of their own. Last but not least are the pastrycook's inventions to suit all tastes, from Provençal Artichoke Pastry to Steak and Kidney Pie.

*Basque Scrambled Eggs
(recipe page 48)*

BASQUE SCRAMBLED EGGS

Piperada con jamón
(photo page 46)

SERVES 4 ■
*Preparation and cooking
    time: 30 minutes
Kcal per portion: 270
P = 16g, F = 21g, C = 5g*

*1 large green pepper
1 large red pepper
3 tbsps olive oil
1 fresh chilli
1 large onion
1 garlic clove
4 tomatoes
1 thyme sprig
1 bay leaf
8 eggs
salt
2 parsley sprigs, chopped*

1. Put the peppers under the grill, or bake them at 250°C/475°F/Gas Mark 9, until the skin begins to brown and blister. Remove them from the heat, cover with a damp cloth and leave to cool a little. Remove the skins, cut the flesh into quarters, removing the seeds, and slice into strips.
2. Heat the oil in a large pan and gently fry the sliced peppers together with the whole chilli. Chop the garlic and onion finely and add them to the pan. Blanch and peel the tomatoes, remove the pips and chop the flesh into cubes. Add them to the vegetables, with the thyme and bay leaf, and season with salt. Cook for 5 minutes, then discard the chilli.
3. Beat the eggs with some salt and the parsley until a very light foam forms, then pour them over the vegetables. Use a wooden spatula to keep the eggs on the move until they just begin to thicken. They should be left creamy. Remove from the heat immediately and serve at once.

ENGLISH FRIED EGGS WITH BACON AND SAUSAGE

SERVES 4 ■
*Preparation and cooking
    time: 20 minutes
Kcal per portion: 485
P = 35g, F = 37g, C = 2g*

*8 mushrooms
4 tomatoes
30g/1oz butter
salt
freshly ground white pepper
8 rashers of streaky bacon
4 eggs
1 tsp oil
4 small pork sausages
watercress sprigs to garnish*

1. Wipe the mushrooms and chop them coarsely. Halve the tomatoes.
2. Heat the plates in a warm oven.
3. In a non-stick frying pan, heat all but a small amount of the butter and fry the tomato halves until the cut surfaces begin to brown; season with salt and pepper. Remove the tomatoes from the pan and keep them hot. Fry the mushrooms in the same fat for 3 minutes, shaking the pan occasionally; season with salt and pepper.
4. Take a second pan and fry the bacon rashers in their own fat until crisp, then set them aside and keep hot. Add a small knob of butter and carefully break four eggs into the pan, without breaking the yolks. Sprinkle with salt and pepper and cook gently until just set. (Alternatively, use a smaller pan and cook the eggs one by one.)
5. Heat the oil in a small pan and fry the sausages until brown and crispy all over, keeping them moving the whole time.
6. Place a fried egg on each of the heated plates with two rashers of bacon beside or

Fry tomatoes and mushrooms in butter and season with salt and pepper.

Fry the bacon rashers in their own fat until crispy.

Fry the eggs one by one in their own pan.

on top of it. Arrange the tomatoes and mushrooms and finally the sausages (without their fat) on the plates. Garnish with a few sprigs of watercress.
Side dish: hot toast.
Recommended drink: strong Ceylon tea.

ITALIAN-STYLE FRIED EGGS

Uova al tegame

SERVES 4 ■
*Preparation and cooking
    time: 20 minutes
Kcal per portion: 325
P = 19g, F = 26g, C = 3g*

*olive oil for the dish
1 onion
1 garlic clove
3 tbsps olive oil
4 ripe beefsteak tomatoes
salt
freshly ground black pepper
pinch of oregano
8 eggs
50g/2oz grated Parmesan
    cheese*

1. Grease a single oval dish or four individual dishes with a little oil. Heat the oven to 200°C/400°F/Gas Mark 6.
2. Dice the onion and garlic fairly finely. Heat the oil in a pan and fry the garlic and onion until they turn transparent.
3. Blanch and peel the tomatoes, remove their seeds and cut the flesh into cubes. Add these to the pan and season with salt, pepper and oregano, then quickly reduce to a thick purée over a high flame.
4. Transfer the tomato sauce to the dish or dishes. Break in the eggs (two per individual dish), taking care not to break the yolks.
5. Bake for a few minutes in the middle of the oven until the egg whites are just firm; the yolks should remain soft. Serve immediately. Put the Parmesan in a small dish so people can sprinkle it on the eggs to suit their own taste.
Side dish: Italian bread (ciabbata).
Recommended wine: a light Italian white, e.g. Frascati.

EGGS IN BURGUNDY SAUCE

Oeufs à la bourguignonne

SERVES 4
*Preparation and cooking
time: 1 hour*
Kcal per portion: 555
P = 21g, F = 30g, C = 6g

100g/4oz streaky bacon
3 shallots
1 carrot
60g/2oz butter
*1 bouquet garni (1 bay leaf, 1
thyme sprig, 2 parsley
sprigs)*
*1 bottle red wine (preferably
a young Burgundy)*
2 cloves
salt
freshly ground black pepper
150g/5½oz mushrooms
8 eggs
1 tsp each butter and flour

1. Dice the bacon. Peel the shallots, scrape or scrub the carrot and dice them both. Heat half the butter in a heavy pan and fry the bacon, carrot and shallots along with the bouquet garni. Add the red wine, cloves and seasoning and simmer for 20 minutes.
2. Meanwhile, wipe the mushrooms with a damp cloth, remove the ends of the stalks and slice the mushrooms thinly. Heat the remaining butter in a pan and fry the mushrooms.
3. Remove the bouquet garni from the red wine and poach the eggs in the liquid in pairs. Slip each egg into the simmering wine in a ladle and immediately roll it so that the egg white fully encloses the yolk. Remove the eggs after 3–4 minutes with a slotted spoon and set them aside in cold water. Use scissors to trim off any filmy traces of egg white.
4. Reduce the red wine over a high heat. Mix the butter and flour together and stir

*Fry the bacon, carrot, shallots
and bouquet garni together. Pour
on the red wine.*

*Remove the poached eggs with a
slotted spoon and set them aside
in cold water.*

into the wine little by little to thicken the sauce. Put the mushrooms in the sauce and season again with salt and pepper.
5. Arrange the poached eggs on a heated plate and pour the sauce over the top.
Side dish: white croûtons or potato pancakes and curly endive or frisée.
Recommended wine: the same Burgundy used for cooking.

SCRAMBLED EGGS WITH TRUFFLES

Uova strapazzate con tartufi

SERVES 2
*Preparation and cooking
time: 10 minutes*
Standing time: 3 hours
Kcal per portion: 325
P = 21g, F = 26g, C = 2g

*1 black truffle (about
15g/½oz), fresh or canned*
4 eggs
2 tbsps double cream
salt
freshly grated nutmeg
4 anchovy fillets, drained
30g/1oz butter

1. Thoroughly wash the truffle, peel and cut it into thin strips or slices. (Reserve the truffle skin for sauce preparation.)
2. Beat the eggs, cream, salt and nutmeg thoroughly with a wire whisk until the mixture begins to foam lightly. Add some liquid from the can if a canned truffle was used. Add the sliced truffle, cover, and leave to stand for 3 hours. Slice the anchovy very finely.
3. Heat 15g/½oz of the butter in a small pan, stir the anchovies around in it for a while, then pour in the egg mixture. Use a wooden spoon to keep the eggs on the move, adding the remaining butter little by little. Remove from the heat as soon as they begin to thicken; the result should remain creamy. Serve as a starter.
Side dish: toast.
Recommended drink: Prosecco.

INDIAN-STYLE SCRAMBLED EGGS

Ekoori

SERVES 4
*Preparation and cooking
time: 20 minutes*
Kcal per portion: 250
P = 14g, F = 20g, C = 2g

1 small onion
*3 tbsps clarified butter or
vegetable oil*
1 fresh green chilli
1 small tomato
*½ tsp peeled, finely grated
fresh ginger root*
*1 tsp finely chopped fresh
coriander*
⅛ tsp turmeric
½ tsp ground cumin
8 eggs
salt
freshly ground white pepper

1. Chop the onion finely. Heat the butter or oil in a pan and cook the onion until soft. Deseed and finely chop the chilli. Blanch and peel the tomatoes, then remove the seeds and chop the flesh coarsely. Add to the onions in the pan, together with the ginger, coriander, turmeric and cumin.

> ### TIP
> *The eggs can be
> served as a filling
> snack in pitta
> bread.*

2. Stir-fry for 3–4 minutes until the tomatoes are soft.
3. Beat the eggs and season lightly with salt and pepper. Pour them into the pan and stir until they thicken; remove from the heat and serve without delay.
Side dish: toast, chapatis or pitta and chutney.

CHINESE PAN-FRIED
EGGS

CHINESE PAN-FRIED EGGS

Mu hsu jou

SERVES 4 ■
*Preparation and cooking
time: 40 minutes
Kcal per portion: 235
P = 7g, F = 11g, C = 6g*

4 eggs
100g/4oz lean diced pork
1 tsp salt
2½ tsp dark soy sauce
1 tsp cornflour
20g/⅝oz dried Chinese
  mushrooms, soaked
200g/7oz Chinese cabbage
4 tbsps oil
1 spring onion
1–2 parsley sprigs
½ tsp monosodium glutamate
  (optional)
½ tsp sake (rice wine)

Scramble the beaten eggs in the wok.

Stir-fry the marinated pork with the spring onion and mushroom until tender.

Fry the coarsely chopped cabbage in the wok.

1. Beat the eggs lightly. Chop the pork finely. Mix together half a teaspoon of salt, half a teaspoon of soy sauce and the cornflour and marinate the meat in it for 10 minutes. Drain the mushrooms in a sieve. Cut larger specimens in half. Trim, wash and coarsely chop the cabbage.
2. Heat two tablespoons of oil in a wok or deep pan and pour in the eggs. Scramble the eggs for 4 minutes over a medium heat. Remove to a plate and keep hot.
3. Trim the spring onion and chop finely. Reheat the wok, pour in the remaining oil and stir-fry the spring onion with the pork and mushrooms for 1 minute. Remove to a plate and keep hot.
4. Stir-fry the cabbage for 1 minute, then cover and fry over a medium heat for a further 5 minutes, stirring from time to time.
5. Return the eggs, meat, onions and mushrooms to the pan and add the parsley.
6. Put half a teaspoon of salt, the soy sauce, the monosodium glutamate (if using) and the sake in the pan. Stir-fry for about 1 minute until the eggs break into pieces.
7. Place in individual Chinese bowls and serve immediately.
Side dish: boiled or fried rice.
Recommended drink: Chinese green tea.

FLORENTINE-STYLE EGGS

Uova alla fiorentina

SERVES 4 ■
*Preparation and cooking
time: 30 minutes
Kcal per portion: 435
P = 32g, F = 33g, C = 3g*

900g/2lbs coarsely chopped
  frozen spinach
6 anchovy fillets
1 garlic clove
3 tbsps oil
salt
freshly grated nutmeg
6 tbsps single cream
8 tbsps grated Parmesan
  cheese
8 eggs
butter for greasing

1. Butter a flat dish or four individual dishes (250ml/9 fl oz each). Heat the oven to 220°C/425°F/Gas Mark 7.
2. Thaw the spinach. Drain and chop the anchovy fillets; chop the garlic clove finely.
3. Heat the oil in a large heavy pan and fry the anchovy fillets and garlic. Add the spinach and fry gently until soft. Season with salt and nutmeg and stir in the cream and 4 tablespoons of Parmesan.
4. Fill the dish or dishes with spinach. Make eight hollows in the spinach bed and carefully break an egg into each one. Sprinkle the eggs and spinach with the remaining Parmesan.
5. Bake for about 10 minutes in the middle of the oven until the egg white is firm. Serve without delay.
Side dish: mashed potato.
Recommended wine: a Tuscan country red.

INDIAN EGGS

Malaidar unday

SERVES 4 ■
*Preparation and cooking
time: 30 minutes
Kcal per portion: 440
P = 16g, F = 40g, C = 4g*

1 small onion
1 small piece of fresh ginger
  root
1 fresh green chilli
1 tsp cumin seeds
3 tbsps oil
250ml/9 fl oz single cream
1 tbsp lemon juice
⅛ tsp cayenne pepper
½ tsp salt
¼ tsp garam masala
2 tsps tomato purée
125ml/4 fl oz chicken stock
6–8 hard-boiled eggs
1 tbsp finely chopped
  coriander or flat parsley

1. Dice the onion finely. Peel the ginger and chop it very finely. Deseed and chop the chilli. Brown the cumin seed in a dry pan, then grind it to a powder.
2. Heat the oil in a large pan. Add the onions and brown lightly. Add the ginger and chilli and fry briefly, then add the cream, lemon juice, cumin, cayenne, salt, garam masala, tomato purée and chicken stock. Mix well and simmer gently.
3. Cut the eggs in half and arrange them, cut sides uppermost, in a layer in the sauce. Spoon the sauce over the eggs and simmer for 5 minutes until the sauce has thickened.
4. Arrange the eggs on a dish, cut sides uppermost and pour the sauce over them. Sprinkle with coriander.
This spicy sauce is also ideal for cauliflower.
Side dish: plain boiled basmati rice.

OMELETTE WITH LOBSTER

Omelette a l'homard

SERVES 2 ■
*Preparation and cooking
    time: 30 minutes
Kcal per portion: 420
P = 31g, F = 32g, C = 1g*

4 eggs
2 tbsps double cream
salt
freshly ground white pepper
20g/¾oz butter
200g/7oz fresh or canned
    lobster meat
2 tbsps sherry or Madeira
2 tbsps crème fraîche
4 tarragon leaves
a little butter to glaze
watercress sprigs to garnish

1. Beat the eggs, cream, salt and pepper thoroughly with a fork until yolks and whites are completely combined.
2. Melt about half the butter in a pan. Break the lobster meat up into small pieces (be sure to drain canned lobster well), and add to the melted butter together with the wine. Add the crème fraîche and tarragon and cook over a medium heat to reduce.
3. Heat the remaining butter in a second pan, pour in the egg mixture and cook quickly, shaking the pan gently, until the resulting omelette is yellow and creamy. Slip the omelette onto a heated plate.
4. Put the lobster filling in the middle of the omelette and fold it over. Glaze with a little butter and garnish with sprigs of watercress.
Serve as a starter for four or as a light main course for two.
Side dish: oakleaf lettuce salad.
Recommended wine: a light dry white.

OMELETTE WITH SORREL

Omelette à l'oseille

SERVES 2 ■
*Preparation and cooking
    time: 15 minutes
Kcal per portion: 305
P = 16g, F = 26g, C = 2g*

2 handfuls of young sorrel
    leaves
40g/1½oz butter
4 eggs
salt
freshly ground white pepper
butter to glaze

1. Wash and drain the sorrel, then remove the stalks – choose young sorrel, with small leaves. Roll up the leaves and cut them into thin strips.
2. Heat 30g/1oz of the butter in a pan and fry the sorrel for 3 minutes. Remove from the heat and set aside to cool.
3. Beat the eggs, salt and pepper thoroughly with a fork until yolks and whites are completely combined. Mix the sorrel with the egg mixture.
4. Heat the rest of the butter in a non-stick pan and tip in the omelette mixture. Shake the pan while cooking the omelette, which should turn out golden and creamy. Put the omelette on a heated plate and glaze with a little butter.
Serve as a starter or snack.
Side dish: two slices of bread, fried in butter.

OMELETTE WITH ROQUEFORT

Omelette au Roquefort

SERVES 2 ■
*Preparation and cooking
    time: 15 minutes
Kcal per portion: 315
P = 21g, F = 25g, C = 1g*

60g/2oz Roquefort cheese
1 tbsp single cream
freshly grated nutmeg
4 eggs
salt
freshly ground black pepper
15g/½oz butter

1. Mash the Roquefort coarsely on a plate with a fork, mix with the cream and season with nutmeg.
2. Using a fork, beat the eggs with a pinch of salt and pepper until yolks and whites are thoroughly combined. Heat the butter in a non-stick pan and pour in the egg mixture. Fry until the omelette is golden in colour.

> **TIP**
>
> *Where possible, always use at least four eggs to make an omelette to prevent it becoming too hard.*

3. Put the cheese mixture in the centre of the omelette and slide it onto a heated plate, then fold up from both sides.
Side dish: young peas seasoned with mint.
Recommended wine: a French red.

OMELETTE WITH SHRIMPS AND MUSSELS

Omelette aux fruits de mer

SERVES 2 ■
*Preparation and cooking
    time: 25 minutes
Kcal per portion: 350
P = 21g, F = 28g, C = 2g*

1 shallot
30g/1oz butter
50g/2oz cooked shelled
    mussels
50g/2oz cooked shelled
    shrimps
1 tbsp white wine
2 tbsps crème fraîche
salt
freshly ground black pepper
1 tbsp chopped parsley
4 eggs
butter to glaze

1. Peel and dice the shallot finely. Heat half the butter in a pan and fry the shallot gently until it turns transparent. Add the shrimps and mussels and fry for just about 1 minute. Pour in the wine and crème fraîche and bring to the boil briefly. Season with salt, pepper and parsley.
2. Using a fork, beat the eggs with a pinch of salt and pepper until yolks and whites are thoroughly combined.
3. Heat the remaining butter in a non-stick pan and tip in the egg mixture. Cook the omelette until it is creamy and golden in colour. Spread the seafood over the soft surface of the omelette, slip it onto a heated plate and fold it in half. Glaze with a little butter.
Side dish: leaf spinach.
Recommended drinks: lager or dry white wine.

TORTILLA WITH ARTICHOKES

Tortilla de alcachotas

SERVES 4 ■
*Preparation and cooking
time: 50 minutes
Kcal per portion: 375
P = 17g, F = 28g, C = 14g*

4 young, closed artichokes
1 onion
2 beefsteak tomatoes
6 tbsps olive oil
salt
8 eggs

Trim the pointed leaves to about half their length.

1. Remove any wilted leaves from the artichokes and trim the pointed leaves to about half their length. Cut the artichokes into thin slices. Peel and dice the onion. Blanch and peel the tomatoes, then dice the flesh and remove the seeds.

TIP

Only the small, closed green or lilac artichokes of the type that reach the markets from the Mediterranean in spring are suitable for this recipe, but canned artichoke hearts may be used at other times.

---

2. Heat 3 tablespoons of oil in a large pan and fry the artichoke and onion, stirring all the time. Add the diced tomato and 2 tablespoons of water. Cover and cook over a medium heat for 10 minutes. Towards the end of this time remove the lid and allow the mixture to sizzle until the vegetables are dry. Season with salt.

Fry the vegetables until the liquid has evaporated, then mix with the eggs.

3. Using a wire whisk, beat the eggs with some salt until yolks and whites are thoroughly combined.
4. Remove the vegetables from the pan and mix with the eggs.
5. Heat 2 tablespoons of the oil in the pan and pour in the vegetable and egg mixture. Stir continuously until the egg begins to thicken. Cover the pan and cook the tortilla over a low heat, shaking the pan occasionally, until the bottom is golden yellow. When it is turned, no liquid egg mixture should remain on the surface of the tortilla.
6. Slide the tortilla onto a plate. Add the remaining tablespoon of oil to the pan and turn the tortilla onto it. Cook this side until it, too, is golden yellow.
Side dish: tomato salad.
Recommended wine: vino tinto.

TORTILLA WITH SPRING VEGETABLES

Tortilla primavera

SERVES 4 ■
*Preparation and cooking
time: 1 hour
Kcal per portion: 305
P = 19g, F = 22g, C = 10g*

500g/1lb 2oz thin green
    asparagus
1 large floury potato
    weighing 150g/5½oz
1 carrot
30g/1oz butter
2 tbsps oil
100g/4oz frozen petits pois
salt
freshly ground black pepper
8 eggs

Carefully fry the potato and carrot slices in the butter and oil.

1. Wash the asparagus thoroughly and cut into 1 cm/½ inch slices; discard the woody ends. Peel the potato, scrub or scrape the carrot and slice them both very thinly.
2. Heat 1 tablespoon of oil and 1 tablespoon of butter in a large non-stick pan. Fry the carrot and potato slices for 10 minutes, stirring all the time with a wooden spoon; do not allow the vegetables to brown. Add the remaining butter, the asparagus and the peas. Fry for a further 10 minutes, stirring all the time. Season with salt and pepper. The vegetables should still be crisp after frying.

Pour the eggs over the vegetables and stir until the eggs begin to thicken.

3. Using a wire whisk, beat the eggs with some salt until yolks and whites are thoroughly combined. Pour it over the vegetables and stir until the eggs begin to thicken. Cover the pan and cook the tortilla over a low heat, shaking the pan occasionally, until the bottom is golden yellow. When it is turned, no liquid egg mixture should remain on the surface of the tortilla. Slide it onto a large plate and turn over.
4. Put the remaining oil in the pan and cook the other side of the tortilla until it is golden yellow. Divide up and serve.
Side dish: lettuce.
Recommended wine: a fruity Spanish or Portuguese rosé.

TIP

Tortillas taste excellent both hot and cold. Instead of these vegetables, use other spring varieties. However, potato should always be among them.

BAKED AUBERGINES WITH MOZZARELLA AND EGGS

Parmigiana di melanzane

SERVES 4 ■■
*Preparation and cooking
   time: 1 hour 30 minutes
Kcal per portion: 665
P = 37g, F = 47g, C = 21g*

*1½kg/3¼lbs aubergines
salt
1kg/2¼lbs sun-ripened
   tomatoes
1 onion
a few fresh basil leaves
freshly ground black pepper
300g/10oz Mozzarella cheese
4 hard-boiled eggs
100g/4oz Parmesan cheese,
   freshly grated*

*flour for tossing
plenty of olive oil for frying
   and for the dish*

Cut the eggs and Mozzarella into thick slices.

After drying the aubergine slices, toss them in flour and fry them in plenty of oil.

1. Brush a rectangular oven-proof dish with oil.
2. Wash the aubergines, slice them lengthways and sprinkle them with salt. Cover with a plate, place a heavy weight on top and leave for 30 minutes.
3. Blanch and peel the tomatoes, then remove the seeds and cut the flesh into cubes. Dice the onion. Heat two tablespoons of oil in a pan and fry the onion until transparent. Shred the basil leaves and add with the tomatoes. Cook gently until reduced to a thick tomato sauce, then season with salt and pepper.
4. Slice the Mozzarella and hard-boiled eggs thickly. Heat the oven to 180°C/350°F/Gas Mark 4.
5. Drain the bitter liquid from the aubergines and dry the slices well on absorbent paper, then toss them in flour. Heat plenty of oil in a deep pan and fry the aubergine slices. Drain well on absorbent paper.
6. Place a layer of aubergine slices in the dish and cover with a sprinkling of grated Parmesan, followed by slices of mozzarella and eggs. Spread a few spoons of tomato sauce over the top, then repeat layers of aubergines, cheese, eggs and sauce until all ingredients have been used up. Finish with tomato sauce.
7. Bake for about 30 minutes in the middle of the oven.
This classic Italian dish tastes excellent hot or cold. The quantity is suitable as a starter for 6-8 people.
Side dish: crusty white bread.
Recommended wines: Pinot Grigio or Chianti.

PROVENÇAL ARTICHOKE PASTRY

Pâté aux artichauts

SERVES 4 ■■
*Preparation and cooking
   time: 1 hour 30 minutes
Kcal per portion: 630
P = 18g, F = 40g, C = 48g*

*300g/10oz frozen puff pastry
8 small closed artichokes
1 onion
1 carrot
2 garlic cloves
250g/8oz mushrooms
5 tbsps olive oil
3 ripe tomatoes
1 thyme sprig
2 tbsps dry white wine
salt
freshly ground black pepper
3 hard-boiled eggs*

*flour for rolling
beaten egg yolk or milk for
   brushing
2 egg yolks
1 tbsp lemon juice
4 tbsps white wine*

1. Thaw the puff pastry for 20 minutes.
2. Wash the artichokes thoroughly. Using a stainless steel knife or scissors, remove the unattractive outer leaves and the small tough leaves on the ends of the stalks. Trim the stalk. Cut the artichokes into quarters and place them immediately in cold water.
3. Peel the onion, scrub or scrape the carrot and cut both into strips. Peel and slice the garlic. Wipe and slice the mushrooms.
4. Heat the olive oil in a stainless steel or enamelled pan. Fry the carrot and onion strips, then add the garlic and artichokes. Fry until tender, stirring all the time, then add the mushrooms. Cook for a further 5 minutes.
5. Blanch and peel the tomatoes, cut them into eighths and remove the seeds and the hard knot where the stalk joins the fruit. Add the flesh to the vegetables, along with the thyme. Pour in the wine, cover and cook for a further 10 minutes. Season with salt and pepper.
6. Heat the oven to 200°C/400°F/Gas Mark 6.
7. Roll out the puff pastry on a floured surface. Cut a long strip to line the tin. Use the rest of the pastry to make a lid for the tin and also a long narrow strip.
8. Put half the artichoke and vegetable mixture into the lined tin. Slice the eggs and arrange in a layer on top. Fill the tin with the rest of the vegetables and cover with the pastry lid. Use the narrow strip to completely seal the pastry case. Brush the top with beaten egg yolk or milk. Cut two small holes in the pastry lid.
9. Bake on the middle shelf of the oven for 40 minutes until golden. Allow to cool slightly.
10. Beat the egg yolks with the lemon juice. Warm the white wine and add it to the mixture, then pour it through the holes in the pastry case.
11. Do not cut the pastry open before it reaches the table.
Side dish: a mixed salad of lamb's lettuce, rocket, young spinach and dandelion.
Recommended wine: a light Provence red.

SHEPHERD'S
PIE

60

SHEPHERD'S PIE

SERVES 4 ■

*Preparation and cooking
   time: 1 hour*
Kcal per portion: 735
P = 31g, F = 51g, C = 36g

1kg/2¼lbs floury potatoes
250ml/8 fl oz milk
50g/2oz butter
1 egg
salt
3 onions
500g/1lb 2oz minced lamb
Worcestershire sauce
100ml/3 fl oz crème fraîche
*extra butter for frying,
   greasing and topping*

*Put the boiled potatoes through a
potato ricer, then add milk, butter
and egg.*

1. Peel the potatoes, cut into even pieces, then boil for about 20 minutes. Drain and allow to steam dry for a while, then put them through a potato ricer, vegetable mill or sieve. Return to the pan, heat gently and stir in the hot milk and butter until a creamy purée results. Beat in the egg and season with salt.

*Season the minced lamb with 1-2
teaspoons of Worcestershire sauce
and the crème fraîche.*

TIP

*Separately
cooked peas can
be added to the
browned mince
before putting it
in the dish.*

*Use a piping bag to lay strips of
potato purée over the meat.*

2. Dice the onions finely. Heat 15g/½oz butter in a pan and fry the onion until it turns transparent. Add the minced lamb, fry quickly until it changes colour, then season with Worcestershire sauce and salt. Add the crème fraîche and simmer for 5 minutes to reduce.
3. Heat the oven to 220°C/425°F/Gas Mark 7.
4. Butter a large shallow dish and fill it with the meat. Put the potato purée in a piping bag and pipe strips of potato over the top of the meat; alternatively, simply spread

the purée over the top and mark with a fork. Dot with butter and bake for 30 minutes in the middle of the oven until golden brown.
Side dish: young peas.
Recommended drinks: beer or a light red wine.

STEAK AND KIDNEY PIE

SERVES 6 ■ ■

*Preparation and cooking
   time: 1 hour 40 minutes*
Kcal per portion: 675
P = 45g, F = 43g, C = 26g

FOR THE PASTRY:
200g/7oz flour
½ tsp salt
100g/4oz butter
3 tsps water

FOR THE FILLING:
1kg/2¼lbs stewing steak
250g/8oz kidney
1 tbsps flour
1 tsp salt
*½ tsp freshly ground black
   pepper*
60g/2oz butter
2 onions
250ml/8 fl oz water
1 bay leaf
2 thyme sprigs

butter for the dish
flour for rolling

1. To make the pastry, sift the flour into a large bowl and sprinkle in the salt. Cut a quarter of the butter into small dice and mix it with the flour. Add the water and quickly knead to a smooth dough.
2. Roll out the pastry on a floured surface. Place another 30g/1oz of diced butter on the pastry. Fold the pastry over twice and roll out again. Repeat the process until all the butter has been used up.
3. Wrap the pastry in aluminium foil and place it in the refrigerator for 30 minutes.
4. Meanwhile trim excess fat from the steak, and cut away the white cores and membranes from the kidneys. Cut both into cubes. Mix the flour with salt and pepper and toss the meat in it; shake off any excess.
5. Heat the butter in a large frying-pan and quickly brown the steak and kidney over a high heat. Remove

*Cover the filling with a pastry lid,
firmly sealed at the edges.*

the meat from the pan and put it in a heavy saucepan. Chop the onions and fry in the meat fat until transparent.
6. Pour the water over the meat and add the bay leaf and thyme. Add the onion sauce, cover, and cook for 1 hour over a low heat.
7. Heat the oven to 220°C/425°F/Gas Mark 7.
8. Grease a long baking tin or dish and fill with the meat. Roll out the pastry on a floured surface. Make a lid the size and shape of the tin or dish and cover the meat with it. Cut any scraps of pastry into strips and place them around the edge of the pie to seal the crust.
9. Bake in the middle of the oven for 10 minutes, then turn the heat down to 175°C/325°F/Gas Mark 3 and bake for a further 20 minutes until the crust is golden brown. Serve immediately.
Side dish: watercress salad.
Recommended drink: a dark beer or country red wine.

Cooking for Special Occasions

*T*he proof that the recipes on the following pages are in the gourmet class can be drawn from the scrambled and stuffed egg recipes which, instead of onions and bacon, use caviar. Although many a gourmet heart will race at the prospect of some of the dishes that follow, they are in no way complicated or time-consuming, nor do they require exclusively expensive ingredients. Curry Gratin with Banana, for example, can be served up within 30 minutes, and unexpected guests can be satisfied with the exquisite Tomato Omelette within a quarter of an hour.
Some of these recipes make wonderful starters – the delicious Mushroom Bake for example, the secret of which is to use newly gathered or bought mushrooms very quickly for that extra fresh flavour.

*Spinach and Carrots au Gratin
(recipe page 74)*

STUFFED EGGS WITH VEGETABLE SALAD

SERVES 4 ■ ■ ■
*Preparation and cooking
    time: 35 minutes*
Kcal per portion: 365
P = 17g, F = 29g, C = 9g

6 eggs
1 large carrot
1 small cauliflower
24 mangetout
½ celeriac
1 oakleaf lettuce
½ sachet unflavoured gelatine
125ml/4 fl oz whipping cream
salt
freshly ground white pepper
30g/1oz keta caviar
20g/¾oz black caviar
40g/1¼oz butter, softened
a little white wine vinegar
olive oil

Mix one portion of whipped cream with keta caviar and the other with black caviar.

Press the yolks of the hard-boiled eggs through a sieve and mix to a smooth paste with butter.

1. Hard boil the eggs. Leave to cool under running cold water.
2. Peel and wash the carrot. Wash and trim the cauliflower and break it into small florets. Cut the ends off the peppers, remove any strings and wash them. Peel the celeriac and cut it into thin slices.
3. Use a small cutter to cut pretty shapes out of the celeriac slices.
4. Boil the carrot whole in salted water, then leave it to cool in the water.
5. Boil or steam the cauliflower florets briefly until firm but tender. Plunge the mangetout into boiling water, then remove them and chill immediately in cold water. Boil the celeriac wafers briefly in salted water and leave them to cool.
6. Wash, clean and drain the oakleaf lettuce.
7. Sprinkle the gelatine into two tablespoons of hot water and stir briskly until thoroughly mixed. Whip the cream and stir the gelatine

into it. Season with salt and pepper and divide into two portions. Mix one portion with the keta caviar and the other with black caviar.
8. Cut the eggs in half lengthways and release the yolks. Place a mound of the caviar cream on each egg half and refrigerate. Press the egg yolk through a sieve, mix to a paste with the softened butter and season with salt and pepper. Refrigerate and serve as an accompaniment to the stuffed eggs.
9. Slice the carrot thinly. Drain the vegetables well. Season with salt, pepper and vinegar and sprinkle with a few drops of oil. Arrange on a serving dish or individual plates with the oakleaf lettuce and eggs.
Side dish: buttered toast.
Recommended wine: a sparkling white.

STUFFED EGGS WITH CAVIAR CREAM AND SALMON

SERVES 4 ■ ■
*Preparation and cooking
    time: 25 minutes*
Marinating time: 1 hour
Kcal per portion: 335
P = 17g, F = 29g, C = 1g

4 eggs
½ sachet gelatine
8 slices fresh salmon (20g/¾oz
    per slice)
100ml/3 fl oz whipping cream
salt
freshly ground white pepper
lemon juice
40g/1¼oz keta caviar
a few dill sprigs

FOR THE MARINADE:
2 tbsps lime or lemon juice
3–4 tbsps olive oil
1 tsp chopped fresh dill

Leave the hard-boiled eggs to cool in water before shelling them.

Mix the gelatine and caviar with the whipped cream.

Release the egg yolks from the egg halves without damaging them.

1. Hard boil the eggs for about 12 minutes. Chill in cold water and leave submerged to cool. Sprinkle the gelatine into two tablespoons of hot water and stir briskly until thoroughly mixed.

> **TIP**
>
> *The egg yolks may be left in the egg and just topped with the caviar cream.*

2. Combine the lemon or lime juice with the olive oil. Lay the salmon slices on a plate, cover with this marinade and sprinkle with dill. Cover with cling film and leave to marinate for one hour.
3. Whip the cream and season with salt, pepper and lemon juice to taste. Mix together the gelatine, caviar and cream.
4. Cut the eggs in half length-

ways and carefully remove the yolk from each.
5. Spread caviar cream over the egg halves and garnish with egg yolks and dill sprigs. Season the salmon with salt and pepper and arrange it with the eggs. Garnish with dill sprigs.
Side dish: vegetable salad.
Recommended wine: Champagne or sparkling white.

EGG AND GOOSE LIVER VOL-AU-VENTS

SERVES 4 ■■

Preparation and cooking time: 30 minutes
Kcal per portion: 555
P = 31g, F = 43g, C = 12g

4 vol-au-vent cases
200g/7oz white meat (veal or poultry)
60g/2oz butter
1 shallot
200g/7oz button mushrooms
250ml/9 fl oz double cream
salt
freshly ground white pepper
oregano
4 eggs
4 slices goose liver terrine, diced

1. Heat the pastry cases in the oven, following the packet instructions.
2. Meanwhile slice the meat into small thin pieces. Heat half the butter in a frying pan and stir-fry the meat until tender. Cover and leave to stand.
3. Heat the remaining butter in a frying pan. Finely chop the shallot, add to the pan and fry until transparent. Wipe and slice the mushrooms, then fry them lightly. Stir in the cream. Simmer until the sauce is smooth and creamy, then season to taste with salt, pepper and oregano.
4. Soft boil the eggs for 6 minutes, cool under running water, then remove the shells and halve the eggs.
5. Take the hot pastry cases out of the oven and fill with the meat and mushroom sauce. Garnish with goose liver and eggs.
Side dish: rice or French bread.
Recommended wines: Gewürztraminer or Riesling.

HAM AND CHEESE BAKE

SERVES 4 ■

Preparation and cooking time: 30 minutes
Kcal per portion: 600
P = 34g, F = 35g, C = 28g

8 slices French bread
250ml/9 fl oz dry white wine
8 slices Emmental cheese, each 3mm/⅛ inch thick
4 slices cooked ham
30g/1oz butter
2 eggs
375ml/15 fl oz milk
salt
freshly ground white pepper
freshly grated nutmeg

1. Heat the oven to 220°C/425°F/Gas Mark 7. If liked, remove the crusts from the bread. Soak the slices in the wine. Top each with slices of cheese and half a slice of ham; arrange in overlapping layers in a buttered ovenproof dish.

> **TIP**
>
> *There is a sweet variation of this in which the cheese and ham are omitted and the beaten eggs and milk are sweetened with sugar. It may also be sprinkled with flaked almonds.*

2. Beat the eggs and milk and season well. Pour half the mixture over the bread in the dish. Bake for about 10 minutes until golden.
3. Pour on the remaining beaten egg and bake for a further 15 minutes until light brown.
Side dish: a mixed salad.
Recommended wine: a dry white.

Remove the crusts from the bread (optional).

Cut the Emmental cheese into eight equal pieces, then into four.

Top each wine-soaked slice of bread with ham and cheese slices.

Pack the bread into a dish and pour on egg and milk mixture.

CURRY GRATIN WITH BANANA

SERVES 4 ■

Preparation and cooking time: 30 minutes
Kcal per portion: 560
P = 18g, F = 43g, C = 26g

4 slices white bread
75g/3oz butter
2 bananas
juice of ½ lemon
4 thin slices of pork fillet
2 tbsps chopped onion
1-2 tbsps curry powder
200ml/6 fl oz single cream
2 tbsp mango chutney
salt
2 tbsps freshly grated mild Cheddar cheese

1. Heat the oven to 220°C/425°F/Gas Mark 7. If liked, remove the crusts from the bread. Heat one-quarter of the butter in a frying pan and fry the bread until bright yellow. Put in an ovenproof dish and set aside in a warm place.
2. Peel and slice the bananas; sprinkle with lemon juice. Add one-third of the remaining butter to the pan and fry the bananas briefly.
3. Heat half the remaining butter, fry the pork and put a slice on each slice of bread. Top with sliced banana.
4. Add the remaining butter to the pan and fry the onion. Add the curry powder, continue cooking for a few minutes, then add the cream.
5. Stir in the mango chutney and add some salt, then simmer to reduce the sauce a little.
6. Pour the sauce over the fried bread and sprinkle with cheese.
7. Bake for about 10 minutes until golden.
Side dish: rice.
Recommended drink: beer.

TOMATO OMELETTE

(photo page 19)

SERVES 4 ■
*Preparation and cooking
    time: 20 minutes
Kcal per portion: 150
P = 7g, F = 13g, C = 1g*

*2 ripe beefsteak tomatoes
2 garlic cloves
8 fresh basil leaves
4 large eggs
2½ tbsps olive oil
pinch of sugar
salt
fresly ground black pepper
1 tsp dried mixed herbs*

1. Slash the skins of the tomatoes, plunge them into boiling water, then into cold water. Remove the skins. Slice the flesh into 1cm/½-inch thick slices and remove the seeds and the hard knot where the stalk joins the fruit.
2. Crush the garlic and chop the basil leaves finely.
3. Beat the eggs until frothy.
4. Heat one tablespoon of the oil in a large frying pan. Add the tomato slices, garlic and half the chopped basil; cook briefly, turning the tomatoes once. Season with sugar, salt, pepper and herbs. Remove the tomatoes from the pan and set aside.
5. Heat one tablespoon of oil in the pan and pour in the beaten eggs. Turn the omelette as soon as they begin to thicken.
6. Top with tomatoes and sprinkle with the remaining oil.
7. Fold the omelette in half and slip it onto a heated plate. Sprinkle with the remaining basil.
Side dish: French bread.
Recommended wines: rioja or chianti.

OMELETTE WITH PRAWNS AND COURGETTES

SERVES 2 ■ ■ ■
*Preparation and cooking
    time: 25 minutes
Kcal per portion: 400
P = 26g, F = 31g, C = 4g*

*100g/4oz cooked peeled
    prawns, fresh or frozen
4 large eggs
5 tbsps single cream
salt
freshly ground black pepper
2 small courgettes
1 fresh green chilli
1 garlic clove
1 tbsp olive oil
15g/½oz butter
1 tsp chopped basil
a few basil leaves to garnish*

1. Thaw frozen prawns for 4–5 hours in the refrigerator.
2. Break the eggs into a bowl. Beat with a fork. Add one tablespoon of cream and season with salt and pepper.
3. Top and tail the courgettes and cut into slices 2.5cm/1-inch thick. Cut the chilli in half lengthways, remove all the seeds and chop the flesh finely. Crush the garlic clove.
4. Heat the oil in a large frying pan. Put in the sliced courgettes and fry, keeping them on the move the whole time. Turn the heat down, cover and continue cooking until the courgettes are just tender. Keep the heat very gentle to prevent juices escaping from the courgettes. Add the chilli and the crushed garlic. Season lightly with salt and pepper.
5. Put the prawns in a sieve and steam over boiling water for a few minutes.
6. Heat the butter in a large pan. Pour in the beaten eggs and cream and allow to thicken slightly, then use a fork to scrape the mixture inwards from the edges, so that all the liquid egg thick-

*Wash and trim the courgettes,
then cut into rings; do not peel
them.*

*Cut the chilli in half lengthways
and remove all seeds.*

ens. Place the omelette on a heated plate while still soft.
7. Heat four tablespoons of cream in a small pan, heat gently and season with a little salt. Mix the prawns with the chopped basil and spread them over the omelette. Pour over the hot cream. Arrange the courgettes as a border. Garnish with a few basil leaves.
Side dish: French bread or toast.
Recommended wine: a dry white.

MINT PANCAKES

SERVES 4 ■
*Preparation and cooking
    time: 20 minutes
Standing time: 1 hour
Kcal per portion: 245
P = 12g, F = 19g, C = 6g*

*6 eggs
3 tbsps flour
4 tbsps milk or single cream
salt
20g/¾oz butter
2 tbsps oil
12 small mint sprigs*

1. Beat the eggs until frothy.
2. Gradually add the flour and stir until a smooth batter is obtained.
3. Add the milk or cream and season with salt. Leave to stand for 1 hour.
4. Melt the butter and stir it into the batter.
5. Wash the mint leaves, dry on absorbent paper and mix with the batter.

> **TIP**
>
> *Depending on the season, the recipe can be varied by using tender basil or sage leaves.
For a sweet variation, sprinkle mint pancakes with sugar.*

6. Heat a little oil in a frying pan and cook four pancakes. Put three mint sprigs on each one before folding it in half. Keep the cooked pancakes hot on a covered plate standing over a pan of hot water, or put them in the oven on the lowest setting until all four are done.
Side dish: tomato salad.
Recommended wine: a light country wine.

MUSHROOM BAKE

SERVES 4 ■■
Preparation and cooking time: 1 hour 15 minutes
Kcal per portion: 455
P = 13g, F = 26g, C = 37g

400g/14oz assorted
   mushrooms
1kg/2¼lbs potatoes
250ml/9 fl oz milk
125ml/4 fl oz single cream
2 eggs, separated
salt
freshly ground black pepper
freshly grated nutmeg
1 onion
1 garlic clove
30g/1oz butter
1 tbsp chopped fresh parsley
1 tbsp chopped fresh
   marjoram
3 tbsps dry white wine
3 tbsps vegetable stock
3 tbsps grated Gruyère or
   Emmental cheese
butter for greasing and
   topping

Skin the boiled potatoes immediately with a sharp knife.

Put the potatoes through a potato ricer.

Spread the mushroom ragout over the bed of seasoned potatoes.

1. Heat the oven to 220°C/425°F/Gas Mark 7. Clean the mushrooms. Cut larger ones in half lengthways.
2. Boil or steam the potatoes in their skins. Allow to cool a little, then peel and put them through a potato ricer or vegetable mill. Mix the potato with the milk, cream and egg yolks. Beat the egg whites until they form stiff peaks and fold into the potato. Season with salt, pepper and nutmeg.
3. Heat the butter in a large pan. Chop the onion and garlic add to the pan and fry gently until transparent. Add the mushrooms and half the parsley and marjoram. Cook over a high heat for 2–3 minutes until the mushrooms have released all their juices.
4. Sprinkle with the wine, allow this to evaporate, then add the stock and continue cooking until the mushrooms are just done. Add the remaining herbs and season with salt and pepper.
5. Butter a fairly deep ovenproof dish. Spread a layer of potato over the bottom of the prepared dish, followed by the mushrooms. Top with a layer of potato.
6. Sprinkle with cheese and dot with butter. Bake in the middle of the oven for 20 minutes.
Side dish: green salad.
Recommended drink: light beer.

AUBERGINES AU GRATIN

SERVES 4 ■
Preparation and cooking time: 1 hour 40 minutes
Kcal per portion: 420
P = 17g, F = 31g, C = 18g

4 medium aubergines
salt
4 tomatoes
freshly ground black pepper
2 tbsps chopped fresh parsley
2 tsps chopped fresh basil
2 garlic cloves
2 green peppers
4 thin slices streaky bacon
2 tbsps olive oil
5 anchovy fillets
200g/7oz Mascarpone cheese

1. Slice the aubergines part way through at 5mm/¼-inch intervals, leaving them hanging together by the skins. Sprinkle with salt and lay them, sliced side down, in a sieve.
2. After 30 minutes wash the aubergines in plenty of cold water, drain them well and pat dry with absorbent paper.
3. Plunge the tomatoes into boiling water, then peel and slice them. Season with salt and pepper, a teaspoon each of parsley and basil and the crushed garlic. Wash the peppers, remove the seeds and pith, then cut them into 25mm/1-inch cubes. Dice the bacon.
4. Heat the oven to 200°C/400°F/Gas Mark 6. Grease a dish with one tablespoon of the olive oil.
5. Arrange the aubergines in the dish. Fill the slits in them with alternate stuffings of tomato slices, bacon and green pepper. Chop the anchovy fillets and scatter them over the top. Finally spread a layer of mascarpone over each aubergine and sprinkle with the remaining olive oil.
6. Cover the aubergines with aluminium foil and bake for about 50 minutes. Remove

Remove the seeds and pith from the peppers, then cut into large cubes.

Arrange the aubergines with their slit sides uppermost in a greased dish.

Stuff the aubergines with vegetables and bacon and spread with mascarpone.

the foil and bake for a further 10 minutes.
7. Sprinkle with the remaining parsley and plenty of pepper and serve at once.
Side dish: risotto.
Recommended wine: an Italian red.

CHICORY AU GRATIN

SERVES 4 ■ ■
Preparation time: 1 hour
Kcal per portion: 270
P = 6g, F = 16g, C = 13

8 chicory heads
150g/5½oz mushrooms
2 tsps lemon juice
200ml/6 fl oz medium dry
    sherry
30g/1oz butter
salt
1 tbsp flour
120ml/4 fl oz single cream
freshly ground white pepper
2 tbsps grated Gruyère cheese
oil or butter for the dish

Wash the chicory thoroughly and cut in half lengthways.

1. Wash the chicory heads thoroughly. Cut 1 cm/½ inch off the ends, then cut each head in half lengthways.
2. Wipe and slice the mushrooms and sprinkle immediately with lemon juice.

> If you find the
> bitter taste of
> chicory heads
> unpleasant,
> make a cone-
> shaped cut in the
> root end when
> preparing it. This
> gives it a milder
> flavour.

3. Put the mushrooms in a small pan with 125ml/4 fl oz of the port and simmer for 5 minutes.
4. Heat 15g/½oz of the butter in a large shallow pan. Add the chicory, sprinkle with salt and pour on the port that was used to cook the mushrooms. Cover and cook gently for 20 minutes.
5. Put 20g/¾oz butter in a small pan, add the flour and cook for 2–3 minutes, without allowing it to brown.
6. Drain the cooking liquid from the chicory and stir it

Place the chicory in hot butter, sprinkle with salt and pour on the sherry.

into the flour in the pan. Add the remaining port and the cream. Simmer gently until slightly thickened, then season with salt and pepper. Heat the oven to 220°C/425°F/Gas Mark 7.
7. Butter a large ovenproof dish. Arrange the well-drained chicory in it. Cover with mushrooms and top with the white sauce. Sprinkle with cheese.
8. Bake for 10 minutes on the middle shelf of the oven until the surface begins to brown.
Side dish: fresh crusty bread.
Recommended wine: rosé.

POTATOES AU GRATIN

SERVES 4-6 ■
Preparation and cooking
*   time: 1 hour 20 minutes*
Kcal per portion: 430
P = 10g, F = 28g, C = 34g

1kg/2¼lbs potatoes
2 garlic cloves
60g/2oz butter
salt
freshly ground white pepper
freshly grated nutmeg
50g/2oz Gruyère cheese,
    grated
200ml/7 fl oz milk
125ml/5 fl oz single cream

Cut the peeled, raw potatoes into thin slices.

1. Choose potatoes that are similar in size. Peel them and cut into thin slices. Crush the garlic.
2. Butter a shallow dish lightly and arrange half the potato slices in the bottom. Sprinkle with salt, pepper and crushed garlic. Top with half the grated cheese and dot with half the remaining butter. Heat the oven to 180°C/350°F/Gas Mark 4.

Season the potato with salt, pepper and nutmeg and sprinkle with Gruyère.

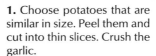

> Vary this recipe
> by mixing some
> steamed leeks
> with the potatoes.
> Or leave out the
> cheese and garlic
> and arrange thin
> slices of apple
> between the
> potato layers.

3. Add the rest of the potatoes and season again. The potato layers should be no deeper than about 4cm/1½ inches.
4. Beat together the milk and cream with some salt, pepper and nutmeg and pour the mixture over the potatoes. Cover with aluminium foil and bake in the middle of the oven.

Pour the seasoned milk and cream over the potatoes and cover with aluminium foil before baking.

5. After 50 minutes raise the oven temperature to 220°C/425°F/Gas Mark 7. Sprinkle the dish with the remaining cheese and dot with the remaining butter. Continue baking for another 20 minutes. Test the potatoes with a fork to see if they are done.
Side dish: green salad.
Recommended wine: a light red.

SPINACH AND CARROTS AU GRATIN

(photo page 62/63)

SERVES 4 ■
*Preparation and cooking
     time: 40 minutes*
Kcal per portion: 335
P = 8g, F = 26g, C = 16g

700g/1½lbs spinach
60g/2oz butter
4 garlic cloves
salt
freshly ground black pepper
6 carrots
4 shallots
½ tsp sugar
250ml/8 fl oz beef stock
200ml/6 fl oz single cream
*3 tbsps fresh white
     breadcrumbs*

1. Wash, trim and coarsely
chop the spinach. Crush the
garlic cloves. Heat 15g/½oz
of the butter in a medium
pan over a low heat. Add the
spinach and garlic. When
the spinach has crumpled,
season with salt and pepper.
2. Scrape or scrub the carrots and cut into slices 3
mm/⅛ inch thick. Chop the
shallots. Heat 30g/1oz of
butter in another pan, add
the carrot slices and shallots
and fry gently for 2–3 minutes. Season with a little salt,
pepper and sugar, then add
the stock.
3. Cook for a few more minutes until the vegetables are
just tender. Heat the oven to
250°C/475°F/Gas Mark 9.
4. Butter an ovenproof dish
and put in the spinach.
Arrange the carrot slices on
top in overlapping layers.
5. Pour in the cream, sprinkle over the breadcrumbs
and dot the surface with the
remaining butter.
6. Bake in the middle of the
oven for about 10 minutes.
Side dish: fried potatoes
Recommended   wine:
Burgundy.

CHARD WITH GREEN SAUCE AU GRATIN

(photo page 23)

SERVES 4 ■■
*Preparation and cooking
     time: 1 hour*
Kcal per portion: 285
P = 7g, F = 25g, C = 9g

1kg/2¼lbs chard
1 tbsp lemon juice
2 shallots
2 garlic cloves
125ml/4 fl oz cream
salt
freshly ground black pepper
2 ripe tomatoes
2 tbsps olive oil
2 tbsps grated Gruyère cheese

1. Remove the leaves from
the chard stalks and set the
leaves aside. Cut the stalks
into small pieces and wash
thoroughly in lemon water.
2. Boil the chard stalks for 15
minutes in salted water.
Remove from the heat and
leave to stand in the liquid.

> ### TIP
>
> *This can be
> turned into a
> satisfying main
> dish by mixing
> diced sausage or
> browned minced
> meat with the
> vegetables. The
> dish can be
> prepared in
> advance and
> simply placed in
> the oven when
> guests arrive.*

3. Put 125ml/4 fl oz of the
cooking liquid in a pan.
Finely chop the shallots and
add to the pan with the
unpeeled garlic cloves. Cook
briskly until the liquid has
reduced by half. Pass
through a sieve into another

*Carefully cut the leaves away from
the stems.*

*Wash one or two of the best
leaves and chop them in a food
processor.*

pan, add the cream and
reduce again, stirring all the
time, until the sauce has a
creamy consistency. Season
with salt and pepper.
4. Wash and finely chop a
few of the best leaves (about
a cupful) and add them to
the sauce.
5. Oil an ovenproof dish and
put the remaining chard in it.
Cover with a layer of sauce.
Heat   the   oven   to
220°C/425°F/Gas Mark 7.
6. Plunge the tomatoes into
boiling water, then peel and
chop coarsely. Drain and fry
briefly in a little oil.
7. Spread a layer of tomatoes over the chard stems,
sprinkle with cheese and put
the dish in the middle of the
oven to bake for 10–15 minutes.
Side dish: potato pancakes.
Recommended wine: a red
country wine.

MUSHROOMS WITH HAM AU GRATIN

SERVES 4 ■■
*Preparation and cooking
     time: 45 minutes*
Kcal per portion: 240
P = 17g, F = 17g, C = 4g

30g/1oz butter
*800g/1lb 12oz button
     mushrooms*
100g/4oz shallots
100g/4oz cooked ham
salt
freshly ground black pepper
200g/7oz full-fat quark
2 egg yolks
freshly grated nutmeg
2 tbsps finely chopped chives

1. Heat   the   oven   to
250°C/475°F/Gas Mark 9.
Butter an ovenproof dish
lightly.
2. Wipe and slice the mushrooms. Peel and finely chop
the shallots. Chop the ham
coarsely.
3. Melt the butter in a large
pan. Fry the shallots until
they turn transparent. Add
the mushrooms and ham
and fry briefly, then season
with salt and pepper.
4. Using a slotted spoon,
transfer the mushroom mixture to the prepared dish.
Boil the juices remaining in
the pan until reduced to
about three tablespoons.
5. Mix the quark with the
egg yolks and season well
with salt, pepper and nutmeg. Stir in the reduced
mushroom liquid.
6. Spread the quark mixture
over the top of the mush-
rooms and bake in the middle of the oven for 5–7
minutes.
7. Sprinkle with chives and
serve.
Side dish: green salad.
Recommended   wines: a
light white or rosé.

Wholefood Recipes

*S*hoots, grains and seeds combine with vegetables and herbs to make savoury crêpes and bakes, starters and main courses to satisfy any appetite. Millet, rye, wheat and lentils are the wholefood ingredients of many of the dishes devised by Doris Katharina Hessler. Eggs are often criticised, but here they come into their own, provided they are produced by hens that forage for themselves in farmyards and fields. Many and varied fresh vegetables have an important part to play: Cauliflower Bake with Bulghur Wheat, Leeks au Gratin with Apple and Sunflower Seeds, and Brussels Sprout, Bean and Potato Bake. All taste as good for brunch as they do later as midday or evening meals.

Cauliflower Bake with Bulghur Wheat (recipe page 90)

CRÊPES WITH SCRAMBLED EGGS AND SMOKED SALMON

SERVES 4 ■ ■
*Preparation and cooking
time: 50 minutes
Kcal per portion: 935
P = 41g, F = 62g, C = 53g*

FOR THE BATTER:
*300g/10oz plain flour
500ml/16 fl oz milk
4 eggs
salt
freshly ground white pepper*

FOR THE TOPPING:
*3 tbsps grapeseed oil
1 tbsp sherry vinegar
salt
freshly ground white pepper
100g/4oz mustard or bean
    sprouts*

FOR THE FILLING:
*4 eggs
125ml/4 fl oz single cream
200g/7oz smoked salmon or
    gravad laks
1 shallot
1 bunch of dill
100g/4oz mustard or bean
    sprouts
salt
freshly ground white pepper*

*4 tbsps oil
40g/1¼oz polyunsaturated
    margarine*

1. Combine the flour, milk and eggs to make a crêpe batter and season with salt and pepper. Leave to rest for 30 minutes.
2. For the topping, mix the oil, vinegar, salt and pepper and marinate the mustard or bean sprouts in this mixture.
3. Begin making the filling by beating the eggs and cream together with a fork. Cut the salmon into small squares; chop the shallot and dill. Mix into the beaten egg along with the mustard or bean sprouts. Season with salt and pepper.

Prepare a crêpe batter by mixing the flour, milk, eggs, pepper and salt.

After the batter has rested for 30 minutes, fry paper-thin crêpes in a little oil.

Mix the chopped salmon into the seasoned beaten egg.

4. Heat a little oil in a non-stick pan. Fry eight crêpes; set aside to keep hot as you make them.
5. Heat the margarine in a second pan and cook the filling over a medium heat until it thickens.
6. Top the crêpes with the scrambled egg filling and serve with a sprinkling of marinated sprouts.
When served as a starter the given quantities are enough for eight.
Recommended   wine: Friulian Pinot Grigio.

BRAISED CHICORY WITH EGG AND CHERVIL

SERVES 4 ■
*Preparation and cooking
time: 30 minutes
Kcal per portion: 225
P = 13g, F = 18g, C = 3g*

*4 small chicory heads
3 tbsps olive oil
salt
freshly ground white pepper
6 hard-boiled eggs
1 bunch of chervil
1 shallot
100ml/3 fl oz yogurt
1 tsp mild mustard*

1. Make a cone-shaped cut in the base of each chicory head and separate the leaves.
2. Heat the olive oil in a large pan and cook the leaves over a high heat. Season with salt and pepper and arrange on a plate in a star pattern.
3. Shell the eggs, cut them in half and remove the yolks. Rub the yolks through a sieve and chop the whites roughly.
4. Chop the chervil finely, reserving a few sprigs for the garnish. Peel and dice the shallot.
5. Combine the egg yolks, yogurt and mustard, then mix in the shallots and chervil. Season well with salt and pepper. Spread the sauce over the chicory leaves, sprinkle with chopped egg white and garnish with chervil.
This starter is also suitable as a light main course, served with wholemeal bread and butter.

FETA CHEESE AND EGG FLAN WITH TOMATO AND BASIL SALAD

SERVES 4 ■ ■
*Preparation and cooking
time: 45 minutes
Kcal per portion: 490
P = 17g, F = 43g, C = 8g*

*250g/8oz Feta cheese
250ml/9 fl oz single cream
3 eggs
2 egg yolks
salt
freshly ground white pepper
butter for the dishes*

FOR THE SALAD:
*4 beefsteak tomatoes
1 bunch basil
2 small shallots
4 tbsps olive oil
1 tbsp garlic vinegar
salt
freshly ground white pepper*

1. Heat the oven to 200°C/400°F/Gas Mark 6. Stand a large shallow pan, partly filled with water, on the middle shelf.
2. Rub the Feta cheese through a sieve and combine it thoroughly with the cream, eggs and egg yolks. Season with pepper and a little salt. Butter four 250ml/8 fl oz soufflé dishes, fill with the mixture and place in the water bath for 25–30 minutes.
3. Meanwhile blanch and peel the tomatoes, then cut them in half, remove the seeds and cut the flesh into small cubes. Pluck the basil leaves from their stalks and set a few aside. Chop the remaining leaves and the shallot finely and mix with the tomatoes. Sprinkle with oil and vinegar, season with salt and pepper and mix well.
4. Turn the flans out onto plates, ring with tomato salad and garnish with basil leaves Serve as a starter.

SOUFFLÉ OF YELLOW PEAS WITH LAMB'S LETTUCE AND CHICK PEA SPROUTS

SERVES 4 ■■
Preparation and cooking time: 1 hour 15 minutes
Kcal per portion: 390
P = 19g, F = 21g, C = 31g

200g/7oz dried yellow split peas
2 eggs, separated
salt
freshly ground white pepper
freshly grated nutmeg
butter for greasing

FOR THE SALAD:
300g/10oz lamb's lettuce
1 bunch chives, finely chopped
200g/7oz chick pea sprouts
2 tbsps apple and honey vinegar
6 tbsps hazelnut oil
salt
freshly ground white pepper
1 shallot, chopped

1. Cook the peas in plenty of unsalted boiling water until tender. Purée 150g/5½oz of the peas with 100ml/3 fl oz of the cooking liquid and then rub through a sieve.
2. Heat the oven to 200°C/400°F/Gas Mark 6. Stand a large shallow pan, partly filled with water, on the middle shelf.
3. Combine the pea purée with the egg yolks, season with salt, pepper and nutmeg and stir in the remaining peas. Whisk the egg whites until they stand in stiff peaks and fold in gently. Divide the soufflé mixture between four buttered 250ml/8 fl oz dishes, which should be filled no more than three-quarters full. Cook in the water bath for 15–20 minutes.
4. Meanwhile, thoroughly wash the lamb's lettuce and

Purée the boiled peas in a blender or food processor.

After puréeing, rub the peas through a fine sieve.

dry thoroughly. Mix it with the chives and chick pea sprouts.
5. Make a dressing by combining the vinegar, hazelnut oil, salt, pepper and shallot. Toss the salad ingredients in the dressing.
6. Turn the soufflés out onto a large plate and arrange the salad around them.
Serve as a starter or light evening meal.

OMELETTE WITH BEAN SPROUTS AND MUSHROOMS

SERVES 4 ■
Preparation and cooking time: 20 minutes
Kcal per portion: 375
P = 19g, F = 32g, C = 2g

200g/7oz shiitake, chanterelles, ceps or button mushrooms
1 shallot
1 bunch chives
50g/2oz butter or margarine
8 eggs
100ml/3 fl oz single cream
200g/7oz bean sprouts
salt
freshly ground white pepper

1. Wipe the mushrooms and cut them into bite-sized pieces. Peel the shallots and chop finely. Chop the chives finely.
2. Heat 20g/¾oz of fat in a pan and cook the shallots and mushrooms briefly over a low heat. Leave to cool a little.
3. Beat the eggs thoroughly with the cream. Stir in the mushrooms, bean sprouts (saving a few of each for the garnish) and chives; season with salt and pepper.
4. Heat the remaining fat in a large heavy pan and pour in the beaten egg. Cook over a medium heat until golden brown on one side, then turn and cook the other side very briefly. Serve with a sprinkling of mushrooms and bean sprouts.
Recommended wine: a light, dry Rheingau Silvaner.

ASPARAGUS WITH EGG AND CHERVIL VINAIGRETTE

SERVES 4 ■■
Preparation and cooking time: 45 minutes
Kcal per portion: 330
P = 15g, F = 30g, C = 8g

800g/1lb 12oz white asparagus
800g/1lb 12oz green asparagus
salt
1 slice white bread
50ml/3 tbsps grapeseed oil
1 tsp sherry vinegar
juice of 1 lemon
4 hard-boiled eggs
1 bunch chervil
100g/4oz capers
50g/2oz well-chilled butter

1. Trim off woody ends and peel off any tough coating from both the green and white asparagus. Put in a large pan with enough salted water to cover, add the bread and boil for 4–6 minutes or until tender but still firm. The bread will absorb any bitterness.
2. Remove the asparagus with a slotted spoon and dry on absorbent paper. Arrange on a serving dish and keep hot. Boil the cooking liquid to reduce it a little, then measure off 200ml/6 fl oz, add the oil, vinegar and lemon juice and boil until reduced by one-third.
3. Shell and chop the eggs. Also chop the chervil, setting aside a few sprigs as garnish. Mix the eggs and chervil into the reduced sauce with the capers. Stir in small pieces of butter while beating with a wire whisk.
4. Pour the sauce over the asparagus and garnish with a few sprigs of chervil. Serve as a starter.

SCRAMBLED EGGS WITH AVOCADO, ROCKET AND ROASTED PINE NUTS

SERVES 4
*Preparation and cooking
    time: 20 minutes
Kcal per portion: 515
P = 17g, F = 46g, C = 9g*

*1 fully ripe avocado
200g/7oz rocket or young
    spinach
1 shallot
6 eggs
50ml/3 tbsps single cream
100g/4oz roasted pine nuts
salt
freshly ground white pepper
40g/1¼oz butter or margarine
    for frying*

1. Peel and halve the avocado, then remove the stone. Cut the flesh into small cubes. Wash the rocket or spinach, dry well, remove the stalks and cut the leaves into thin strips. Peel and finely chop the shallot.
2. Beat the eggs and cream thoroughly with a fork and mix in the avocado, rocket or spinach, shallot and pine nuts. Season with salt and pepper.
3. Heat the fat in a non-stick pan and scramble the eggs, stirring carefully. They should be thick, but still moist and shiny. Divide up and serve as a starter or light evening meal.
Side dish: tender green salad.

SCRAMBLED EGGS WITH GRAVAD LAKS, CUCUMBER AND DILL

SERVES 4
*Preparation and cooking
    time: 20 minutes
Kcal per portion: 465
P = 34g, F = 35g, C = 2g*

*400g/14oz gravad laks
1 small cucumber
1 bunch dill
6 eggs
50ml/3 tbsps single cream
200g/7oz mustard or bean
    sprouts
salt
freshly ground white pepper
3 tbsps grapeseed oil*

1. Cut the salmon into small squares. Wash the cucumber, cut in half and scrape the pips out with a spoon, then cut the halves into small cubes, leaving the skin on. Remove the stalks from the dill and chop finely (reserve a few leaves for the garnish).

TIP

*Instead of gravad
laks, smoked
salmon or any
other smoked fish
makes a suitable
substitute.*

2. Beat the eggs and cream thoroughly. Mix in the fish, cucumber, dill and mustard or bean sprouts and season with salt and pepper.
3. Heat the oil in a frying pan, pour in the beaten egg and scramble over a medium heat, stirring all the time. Arrange on plates and garnish with dill.

Cut the gravad laks or smoked salmon into small cubes with a sharp knife.

Use a small spoon to scrape the pips out of each half of the cucumber.

Scramble the eggs over a medium heat, stirring all the time.

SCRAMBLED EGGS WITH TOMATOES, GARLIC AND BASIL

SERVES 4
*Preparation and cooking
    time: 20 minutes
Kcal per portion: 250
P = 12g, F = 21g, C = 3g*

*2 beefsteak tomatoes
2 garlic cloves
1 shallot
2 bunches of basil
6 eggs
50ml/3 tbsps single cream
salt
freshly ground white pepper
3 tbsps olive oil*

1. Blanch and peel the tomatoes, cut them in half and remove the seeds; finally cut them into small cubes, discarding the hard knot where the stalk joins the fruit. Peel the shallot and garlic. Crush the garlic with the side of a large knife; chop the shallot and basil finely. Set aside a few chopped tomatoes and basil leaves for the garnish.

TIP

*The scrambled
eggs may be
sprinkled with a
little freshly
grated Parmesan
cheese.*

2. Beat the eggs and cream thoroughly with a fork and stir in the ingredients already prepared. Season with salt and pepper.
3. Heat the oil in a non-stick pan, pour in the beaten egg and scramble over a medium heat, stirring all the time. Arrange the scrambled eggs on heated plates and garnish with the reserved tomatoes and basil leaves.
Side dish: toast.

MILLET PANCAKES STUFFED WITH SPINACH AND CHEESE

SERVES 4 ■■
Preparation and cooking time: 45 minutes
Kcal per portion: 750
P = 32g, F = 49g, C = 45

FOR THE BATTER:
200g/7oz millet flour
300ml/12 fl oz milk
3 eggs
salt
freshly ground white pepper
polyunsaturated margarine for frying

FOR THE STUFFING:
1kg/2¼lbs young spinach
salt
80g/3oz pine nuts
150g/5½oz Emmental cheese
2 small shallots
40g/1½oz polyunsaturated margarine
freshly ground white pepper
freshly grated nutmeg
100ml/3 fl oz single cream

1. Make a smooth pancake batter out of the millet flour, milk and eggs and season with salt and pepper. Leave to rest for 30 minutes.
2. Meanwhile, wash the spinach thoroughly and blanch for about 2 minutes in a little salted water. Leave to drain thoroughly.
3. Roast the pine nuts in a dry non-stick pan. Cut the Emmental into small cubes.
4. Peel and dice the shallots. Heat the margarine in a large pan. Fry the shallots gently until transparent, then add the spinach, continue frying and season with salt, pepper and nutmeg. Stir in the cream, then add the pine nuts and cheese cubes. Bring to the boil, then immediately set aside.
5. Heat a little margarine in a large non-stick pan and fry four thin pancakes.

Make a smooth batter out of the millet, milk and eggs.

After washing the spinach, blanch it in salted water for 2 minutes.

Drain the spinach thoroughly in a sieve before further cooking.

6. Spread an even layer of the spinach mixture over each pancake, fold in half and serve immediately.
Side dish: cheese or cream sauce.
Recommended wine: dry Italian white, e.g. Sauvignon.

MILLET SOUFFLÉS WITH VEGETABLES

SERVES 4 ■■
Preparation and cooking time: 50 minutes
Kcal per portion: 270
P = 10g, F = 12g, C = 29g

50g/2oz each carrot, fennel and leek
salt
150g/5½oz boiled millet flakes or grains
50ml/3 tbsps crème fraîche
3 eggs, separated
freshly ground white pepper
oil and breadcrumbs for the dishes

1. Clean and dice the vegetables. Blanch in salted, boiling water, chill under cold water and drain in a sieve.
2. Heat the oven to 200°C/400°F/Gas Mark 6. Place a shallow pan, partly filled with hot water, on the middle shelf.
3. Purée 100g/4oz boiled millet with the crème fraîche, then rub through a sieve. Mix in the whole millet, the chopped vegetables and the egg yolks. Season with salt and pepper. Beat the egg whites stiffly and fold into the mixture.
4. Prepare four 250ml/7 fl oz soufflé dishes by coating with oil and sprinkling with breadcrumbs. Divide the mixture between the dishes. (Alternatively, fill a single 1.5l/2¼-pint soufflé dish.) Stand the dishes or dish in the water bath and cook for 15–20 minutes. Serve immediately.
Serve the soufflés as a starter with a herb or cream sauce, or as an accompaniment to game.

WHOLEMEAL PANCAKES WITH CHINESE VEGETABLES

SERVES 4 ■■
Preparation and cooking time: 40 minutes
Kcal per portion: 605
P = 24g, F = 23g, C = 64g

FOR THE BATTER:
300g/10oz wholemeal flour
4 eggs
500ml/16 fl oz milk
salt
freshly ground white pepper
polyunsaturated margarine for frying

FOR THE FILLING:
100g/4oz each carrots, fennel, leek, Chinese cabbage, onion and mushrooms
100g/4oz bean sprouts
4 tbsps sesame oil
2 garlic cloves, crushed
50g/2oz fresh ginger root, grated
1 tsp honey
½ tsp sambal oelek
salt
freshly ground white pepper
100ml/3 fl oz each soy sauce, sherry and sake
40ml/3 tbsps sherry vinegar

1. Beat together the flour, eggs and milk. Leave to rest for 30 minutes.
2. Prepare all the vegetables, cut into fine strips and mix with the bean sprouts.
3. Heat the oil in a wok and stir-fry the vegetables over a medium heat. Add all the other ingredients and continue to stir-fry for 3–4 minutes.
4. Heat a little margarine in a frying pan and fry four thin pancakes. Fill the pancakes with the vegetables, fold in half and serve.
Recommended wine: a dry white, e.g. a Loire valley Pouilly-Fumé.

CHINESE CABBAGE AND ROASTED PISTACHIO SOUFFLÉ

SERVES 4 ■■
*Preparation and cooking
    time: 1 hour
Kcal per portion: 590
P = 37g, F = 44g, C = 11g*

750g/1lb 10oz Chinese
    cabbage
3 tbsps oil
salt
freshly ground white pepper
500g/1lb 2oz quark
125ml/4 fl oz single cream
3 eggs, separated
freshly grated nutmeg
100g/4oz roasted pistachios
    nuts, chopped
butter for the dish
100–150g/4–5oz grated
    Cheddar cheese

1. Cut the Chinese cabbage in half, remove the hard stem, wash and cut into fine strips. Heat the oil in a large pan and fry the cabbage strips briefly. Season with salt and pepper.
2. Heat the oven to 200°C/400°F/Gas Mark 6.
3. Combine the quark, cream and egg yolks; season with salt, pepper and nutmeg. Add a pinch of salt to the egg whites and beat them until stiff, then fold into the quark mixture.
4. Grease a large dish or deep soufflé dish and fill with half the quark mixture. Cover with a layer of cabbage and sprinkle with the pistachios. Spread the remaining quark over this and top with grated cheese.
5. Bake to a golden brown in the middle of the oven for 25–30 minutes, then serve immediately to avoid the soufflé collapsing.
Recommended wine: a lightly aromatic white, e.g. Müller-Thurgau.

VEGETABLE SOUFFLÉS

SERVES 4 ■■
*Preparation and cooking
    time: 40 minutes
Kcal per portion: 200
P = 8g, F = 16g, C = 6g*

250g/8oz cooked vegetable
    (carrots, celery, peas or
    fennel)
100ml/3 fl oz crème fraîche
3 eggs, separated
salt
freshly ground white pepper
butter and breadcrumbs for
    the dishes

1. Heat the oven to 200°C/400°F/Gas Mark 6. Place a large shallow pan, partly filled with water, on the middle shelf.
2. Purée the cooked vegetable with the crème fraîche and egg yolks, then rub through a sieve and season with salt and pepper. Beat the egg whites until they stand in stiff peaks and carefully fold them into the vegetable purée.

TIP

This is a basic recipe that can be varied with the seasons according to the vegetables available. Use appropriate herbs for the vegetable being used, e.g fennel tops for fennel, carrot tops for carrots, dill for courgettes etc.

---

3. Butter four 250ml/9 fl oz dishes and sprinkle with breadcrumbs. Spoon in the purée but do not fill higher than three-quarters full. Cook in the water bath in the oven for about 25 minutes.

Cook the carrots, celery, peas or fennel in advance.

Purée the vegetable with the crème fraîche and rub through a sieve.

Beat the egg whites in the food processor until they stand in stiff peaks.

Serve as a side dish with fish, meat or poultry, or as a starter with a herb sauce.

BROCCOLI, SPINACH AND BULGHUR WHEAT AU GRATIN

SERVES 4 ■■■
*Preparation and cooking
    time: 1 hour
Kcal per portion: 735
P = 32g, F = 50g, C = 37g*

1kg/2¼lbs young spinach
salt
2 small shallots
40g/1½oz polyunsaturated
    margarine
200g/7oz bulghur wheat
250ml/8 fl oz single cream
freshly ground white pepper
freshly grated nutmeg
500g/1lb 2oz broccoli
250ml/8 fl oz vegetable stock
20ml/1 tbsp dry sherry
20ml/1 tbsp sherry vinegar
3 egg yolks
200g/7oz Emmental cheese,
    grated

1. Wash and trim the spinach, then blanch in salted, boiling water for 1 minute. Chill in cold water then squeeze out well.
2. Peel and finely chop the shallots. Heat the margarine in a pan and fry the shallots gently. Add the spinach, fry briefly, then add the bulghur wheat and half the cream. Season to taste.
3. Wash the broccoli and break it into florets; blanch in salted water.
4. Put the stock in a heavy pan with the remaining cream, sherry and vinegar and boil until reduced by about one-third. Remove from the heat and mix in the egg yolks.
5. Fill an ovenproof dish with the spinach mixture and top with well-drained broccoli. Sprinkle with cheese and pour over the cream sauce.
6. Brown for a few minutes under the grill.
Recommended wine: south German Spätburgunder.

LEEKS AU GRATIN WITH APPLE AND SUNFLOWER SEEDS

SERVES 4 ■
Preparation and cooking time: 1 hour 10 minutes
Kcal per portion: 780
P = 34g, F = 62g, C = 21g

4 leeks
1 cooking apple
4 tbsps grapeseed oil
salt
freshly ground white pepper
200g/7oz sunflower seeds
200g/7oz quark
200ml/6 fl oz single cream
6 eggs
freshly grated nutmeg
butter for the dish

Fry the sliced leeks over medium heat and add the apples.

Roast the sunflower seeds in a dry pan, stirring constantly.

Beat the quark, eggs and cream thoroughly with a wire whisk.

1. Remove the root and the tough green leaves from the leeks. Cut into fine rings, wash and drain in a sieve. Peel the apple and then slice thinly.
2. Heat the oven to 200°C/400°F/Gas Mark 6.
3. Heat the oil in a pan and fry the leeks over a medium heat, then season and mix with the apple.
4. In a dry non-stick pan, roast the sunflower seeds.
5. Combine the quark, cream and eggs and season well with salt, pepper and nutmeg.
6. Butter a large ovenproof dish. Put in the leek and apple mixture, sprinkle with sunflower seeds and top with the cheese mixture. Bake in the middle of the oven for 35–40 minutes until golden-brown.
Recommended wines: a light dry Riesling, e.g. a Mosel or Rheingau.

SAVOY CABBAGE AND SWEETCORN BAKE

SERVES 4 ■ ■
Preparation and cooking time: 1 hour 15 minutes
Kcal per portion: 380
P = 17g, F = 20g, C = 32g

250ml/9 fl oz milk
50g/2oz cornmeal
salt
freshly ground white pepper
half a Savoy cabbage (400g/14oz when prepared)
1 onion
3 tbsps grapeseed oil
200g/7oz can sweetcorn
4 eggs, separated
200ml/6 fl oz yogurt
fat and breadcrumbs for the dish

Heat the milk and gradually add the cornmeal, stirring constantly.

Fold the stiffly beaten egg whites into the vegetable, cornmeal and yogurt mixture.

Butter a soufflé dish generously and sprinkle with breadcrumbs.

Fill the dish with the mixture and bake for about 30 minutes.

1. Bring the milk to the boil and stir in the cornmeal a little at a time. Season with salt and pepper and leave over a low heat for 30 minutes, stirring from time to time.
2. Cut the cleaned Savoy cabbage and the onion into fine strips. Heat the grapeseed oil in a large pan and fry the strips over a medium heat. Drain the sweetcorn, add to the pan and season with salt and pepper.
3. Heat the oven to 200°C/400°F/Gas Mark 6.
4. Stir the egg yolks and yogurt into the cornmeal and mix in the vegetables. Beat the egg whites together with a pinch of salt until they stand in stiff peaks, then fold them carefully into the mixture.
5. Butter a soufflé dish and scatter breadcrumbs over the surface. Fill with the soufflé mixture and bake in the middle of the oven for 25–30 minutes.
Side dish: herb sauce.
Recommended wine: strong, dry south German Grauburgunder.

CAULIFLOWER BAKE WITH BULGHUR WHEAT

(photo page 76/77)

SERVES 4 ■ ■
*Preparation and cooking
time: 1 hour
Kcal per portion: 540
P = 17g, F = 35g, C = 40g*

*1 small cauliflower
salt
4 tomatoes
1 bunch basil
1 onion
2 garlic cloves
200g/7oz bulghur wheat
125g/5oz Mascarpone cheese
250ml/8 fl oz single cream
2 eggs
freshly ground white pepper
freshly grated nutmeg*

1. Wash and trim the cauliflower. Break into small florets and cut stalks and stem into small cubes. Blanch for 2–3 minutes in boiling salted water, then drain in a sieve.
2. Heat the oven to 200°C/400°F/Gas Mark 6.
3. Blanch and peel the tomatoes, then cut them in half, remove the seeds and finally dice the flesh. Chop the basil. Dice the onion and crush the garlic.
4. Mix the cauliflower with these ingredients and add the bulghur wheat; butter a soufflé dish and fill with this mixture.
5. Combine the Mascarpone, cream and eggs and season with salt, pepper and nutmeg. Spread over the other ingredients and bake for about 30 minutes in the middle of the oven.
Recommended wine: a dry rosé.

BRUSSELS SPROUT, BEAN AND POTATO BAKE

SERVES 4 ■ ■
*Preparation and cooking
time: 1 hour 10 minutes
Kcal per portion: 755
P = 39g, F = 49g, C = 39g*

*200g/7oz dried black beans
500g/1lb 2oz small Brussels
   sprouts
salt
200g/7oz waxy potatoes
250g/8oz mature Cheddar
   cheese
2 garlic cloves
butter for the dish
250ml/9 fl oz single cream
2 eggs
freshly ground white pepper
freshly grated nutmeg*

1. Boil the beans until nearly tender in plenty of unsalted water. Wash and trim the Brussels sprouts and blanch in salted, boiling water. Peel and wash the potatoes, then cut them into paper-thin slices.
2. Heat the oven to 200°C/400°F/Gas Mark 6. Grate the cheese.
3. Peel the garlic cloves and cut in half. Rub them over a large ovenproof dish. Butter the dish generously and spread with alternating layers of well-drained beans, Brussels sprouts and potatoes. Sprinkle a little cheese between each layer.
4. Beat the cream and eggs together thoroughly and season with salt, pepper and nutmeg; pour this mixture over the other ingredients in the dish. Bake in the middle of the oven for 25–30 minutes until golden-brown.
Recommended wine: a light red.

Boil the beans in unsalted water. Cooking time can be reduced if the beans are soaked overnight.

Slice the raw potatoes.

Layer the beans, potatoes and sprouts in a buttered ovenproof dish.

CURRIED LENTILS AU GRATIN

SERVES 4 ■
*Preparation and cooking
time: 25 minutes
Kcal per portion: 515
P = 15g, F = 37g, C = 32g*

*1 onion
3 tbsps sunflower oil
200g/7oz cooked lentils
100g/4oz bean sprouts
50g/2oz desiccated coconut
100g/4oz roasted pine nuts
20g/¾oz fresh root ginger,
   grated
2 tsps ground turmeric
¼ tsp ground cumin
salt
freshly ground white pepper
butter for the dish
4 egg yolks
50ml/3 tbsps single cream*

1. Heat the oven to 200°C/400°F/Gas Mark 6.
2. Dice the onion and sweat it in oil in a heavy pan. Add the lentils, bean sprouts, coconut and pine nuts and fry briefly. Add all the spices, season to taste and heat thoroughly.

> **TIP**
>
> *This dish can be put under the grill to brown for a few minutes.*

3. Butter an ovenproof dish and fill with the mixture. Beat the egg yolks and cream together and pour over the dish. Bake for 10 minutes in the middle of the oven.
Side dish: mixed salad.
Recommended wine: an aromatic wine, e.g. a Muscatel.

Quick-and-easy Recipes

*J*ust about any meal made with eggs will come out top in a speed trial. So there is no need to wilt under the onslaught of unexpected guests and retire to a restaurant or raid the refrigerator for boring cold cuts.

Scrambled Eggs with Mushrooms or Boiled Eggs Tartar, Minced Steak with Eggs or Eggs in Beefsteak Tomatoes are far worthier alternatives. Lovers of baked dishes are also well served in this chapter. Baked Tagliatelle with Chicken Breast can be served within 30 minutes, and Baked Leeks with Garlic Sausage takes only 5 minutes longer. Among the other dishes that will make it to the table in under half an hour are Baked Sauerkraut and Liver Sausage, and Tuna and Rigatoni au Gratin.

Oriental Rice Bake
(recipe page 100)

SCRAMBLED EGGS WITH MUSHROOMS

(photo page 17)

SERVES 4 ∎
*Preparation and cooking
time: 25 minutes
Kcal per portion: 385
P = 16g, F = 32g, C = 1g*

200g/7oz smoked streaky
  bacon rashers
3 spring onions
2-3 tbsps oil
500g/1lb 2oz mushrooms
6 eggs
5 tbsps single cream
salt
*freshly ground black pepper
chopped chives (optional)*

1. Remove the rind and cut the streaky bacon into fine strips.
2. Wash and trim the spring onions and cut them into fine rings.
3. Heat half the oil in a large non-stick pan. Fry the bacon over a low heat until the fat runs out, then add the spring onions.
4. Wipe the mushrooms and slice them finely. Add them to the pan and fry until nearly all the juices have evaporated, adding more oil if necessary.
5. Beat the eggs thoroughly with the cream, add plenty of salt and pepper and pour over the mushrooms. Slowly scramble the eggs over a gentle heat, stirring all the time. Sprinkle with chopped chives if desired. To save a few calories, simply leave out the bacon.
Side dish: crusty bread.
Recommended drink: beer.

EGGS IN BEEFSTEAK TOMATOES

SERVES 4 ∎
*Preparation and cooking
time: 25 minutes
Kcal per portion: 305
P = 20g, F = 24g, C = 4g*

4 large ripe beefsteak
  tomatoes
salt
freshly ground black pepper
1 tsp fresh or dried oregano
200g/7oz cooked ham, sliced
  thickly
4 eggs
4 tsps grated Parmesan
  cheese
30g/1oz butter
2 tbsps olive oil
1 tbsp red wine vinegar

1. Wash the tomatoes and remove their tops. Scoop out the pips and some of the flesh with a teaspoon. Purée the tops and the flesh.
2. Season the hollowed-out tomatoes on the inside with salt, pepper and a sprinkling of oregano.
3. Cut the ham into fine strips, discarding any fat, and divide it between the tomatoes.
4. Heat the oven to 180°C/350°F/Gas Mark 4.
5. Break an egg into each tomato and sprinkle with Parmesan and a pinch of salt. Dot with butter.
6. Put on a baking tray or in a shallow dish and bake in the middle of the oven for 12–15 minutes.
7. Meanwhile, season the puréed tomato flesh with olive oil, vinegar, salt and pepper. Serve with the tomatoes.
Side dish: French bread.
Recommended wine: a light French or Italian red.

Scoop out the pips and some of the flesh with a spoon.

Purée the tops and the flesh.

Season the scooped-out tomatoes and add the strips of ham.

Break an egg over the ham and sprinkle with Parmesan.

BOILED EGGS TARTAR

SERVES 4 ∎
*Preparation and cooking
time: 20 minutes
Kcal per portion: 210
P = 12g, F = 17g, C = 4g*

6 eggs
1 onion
5 gherkins
1 red pepper
4 tbsps mayonnaise
3 tsps English mustard
salt
freshly ground white pepper
pinch of cayenne
2 garlic cloves
1 bunch chervil

1. Hard boil the eggs for 10 minutes, then chill them in cold water, remove the shells and leave to cool.
2. Chop the onion finely and put it in a bowl. Chop the gherkins, deseed and chop the red pepper. Add to the bowl.
3. Cut the eggs into small cubes with an egg cutter or small sharp knife and place them in the bowl with the other ingredients.
4. Combine the mayonnaise and mustard. Season with salt, pepper and cayenne. Peel and crush the garlic cloves; add to the mixture. Combine the mayonnaise with the egg tartar.
5. Wash the chervil and remove the stalks; chop the leaves finely and stir into the tartar.
Side dish: fresh crusty bread or jacket potatoes.
Recommended drink: beer.

MINCED STEAK WITH EGGS

SERVES 4
Preparation and cooking
time: 25 minutes
Kcal per portion: 280
P = 39g, F = 13g, C = 3g

1 onion
1 tbsp olive oil
2 garlic cloves
600g/1lb 6oz minced steak
3 tbsps tomato purée
150g/5½oz Feta cheese
1 tsp fresh or dried oregano
salt
frshly ground black pepper
pinch of cayenne
4 eggs

1. Dice the onion finely. Heat the oil and fry the onion until it turns transparent. Crush the garlic cloves into the pan.
2. Mix in the minced steak and fry until it takes on a crumbly texture.
3. Add the tomato purée. Crumble the cheese over the pan. Mix together well and season with oregano, salt, pepper and cayenne.
4. Smooth the surface of the minced meat and, using the back of a spoon, make four hollows in the surface. Break an egg into each hollow.
5. Cover the pan and cook the eggs over a medium heat for about 6 minutes.
Side dish: sesame seed bread and cucumber salad with garlic.
Recommended wine: retsina or a dry Greek wine.

Mix the minced steak with the onion and garlic and fry until crumbly.

Crumble the cheese over the pan, stir and season well.

Use a spoon to make four hollows in the smooth surface of the meat.

Break an egg into each of the hollows, cover the pan and cook for 5–6 minutes.

POACHED EGGS IN HERB SAUCE

SERVES 4
Preparation and cooking
time: 25 minutes
Kcal per portion: 250
P = 21g, F = 17g, C = 3g

1 onion
15g/½oz butter
2 garlic cloves
250ml/8 fl oz stock
200g/7oz fresh cream cheese
   with herbs
1 bunch of mixed herbs or a
   bunch each of parsley,
   basil, dill and chives
125ml/4 fl oz white wine
   vinegar
salt
8 eggs
freshly ground white pepper
freshly grated nutmeg
2 tbsps lemon juice

1. Dice the onion. Melt the butter and fry the onion until it turns transparent.
2. Crush the garlic into the pan.
3. Pour in the stock and add the cream cheese. Stir and simmer until the cheese has melted. Keep warm.
4. Wash the herbs, pat them dry and chop finely.
5. In a large pan, bring about 1.5l/2½ pints of water to the boil with salt and vinegar added. Break the eggs one by one into a cup, and slip them into the boiling water. Simmer for about 5 minutes until cooked. (You may prefer to cook the eggs in two batches.)
6. Season the cheese sauce with salt, pepper, nutmeg and lemon juice and stir in the herbs.
7. Lift the eggs out with a slotted spoon, arrange them on plates and pour over the sauce.
Side dishes: new potatoes boiled or steamed in their skins and green salad.
Recommended wine: a light white.

GORGONZOLA EGGS IN TOMATO CREAM

SERVES 4
Preparation and cooking
time:
30 minutes
Kcal per portion: 615
P = 29g, F = 50g, C = 11g

8 eggs
30g/2oz butter
2 tbsps flour
250ml/9 fl oz milk
300g/10oz passata (puréed
   tomatoes)
2 garlic cloves
200ml/6 fl oz single cream
salt
freshly ground black pepper
1 tsp fresh or dried thyme
200g/7oz Gorgonzola or
   Dolcelatte cheese
fresh basil to garnish

1. Hard boil the eggs for 10 minutes, then chill in cold water.
2. Heat the butter in a heavy pan, sprinkle in the flour and cook gently until it turns yellow. Pour in the tomatoes and milk and simmer for 5 minutes, stirring occasionally.
3. Heat the oven to 200°C/400°F/Gas Mark 6.
4. Crush the garlic into the sauce, stir in the cream and season with salt, pepper and thyme.
5. Shell the eggs, cut them in half lengthways and remove the yolks. Mix the yolks to a creamy paste with the cheese, season with pepper, and spoon into the halved eggs.
6. Pour the tomato cream into a dish, or individual dishes, and arrange the eggs in it. Bake for 15 minutes in the middle of the oven.
7. Garnish liberally with basil leaves before serving.
Side dish: French bread.
Recommended wine: a strong red, e.g. Rioja or Burgundy.

TUNA AND RIGATONI AU GRATIN

SERVES 4 ■

Preparation and cooking time: 30 minutes
Kcal per portion: 825
P = 48g, F = 29g, C = 91g

500g/1lb 2oz rigatoni
salt
2 x 150g/5½oz cans tuna in brine
400g/14oz can tomatoes
freshly ground black pepper
100g/4oz stoned black olives
1 tsp fresh or dried oregano
butter for the dish
300g/10oz Mozzarella cheese

1. Cook the rigatoni in salted, boiling water until just al dente. Drain well in a sieve.
2. Drain the tuna and break it up with a fork.
3. Mix the tomatoes and their juice with the tuna, breaking up the tomatoes with a fork. Season with salt and pepper and add the olives and oregano.
4. Heat the oven to 220°C/425°F/Gas Mark 7.
5. Butter a large ovenproof dish and fill it with the pasta. Spread the sauce over the top.
6. Slice the Mozzarella thinly and place it in overlapping layers over the dish. Sprinkle with pepper.
7. Bake in the middle of the oven for 20 minutes, until the cheese has melted.
Side dish: mixed salad with vinaigrette dressing.
Recommended wine: an Italian red.

PASTA AND LEEK BAKE

SERVES 4 ■

Preparation and cooking time: 30 minutes
Kcal per portion: 725
P = 38g, F = 26g, C = 85g

500g/1lb 2oz small pasta shapes
salt
200g/7oz leeks
30g/1oz butter
freshly ground black pepper
200g/7oz cooked ham, thickly sliced
150g/5½oz Cheddar cheese

1. Cook the pasta in salted boiling water until just al dente and drain well in a sieve.
2. Trim the leeks, slit open lengthways and cut into thin rings. Wash and drain thoroughly.
3. Heat half the butter in a pan and fry the leeks gently for 3 minutes. Season with salt and pepper.
4. Cut the ham into strips, discarding the fat. Add the strips to the leeks and mix well.
5. Heat the oven to 200°C/400°F/Gas Mark 6. Grate the cheese coarsely.
6. Grease an ovenproof dish with the remaining butter. Fill with alternating layers of pasta and leek and ham, sprinkling each layer with a little cheese. Top with a generous layer of cheese.
7. Bake in the middle of the oven for 15 minutes.
Side dish: green salad with yogurt dressing.
Recommended drinks: beer or dry white wine.

Fry the sliced leeks gently in a little butter.

Cut the ham into strips and mix with the leeks.

Place alternate layers of pasta, leeks and ham in a buttered ovenproof dish.

BAKED TAGLIATELLE WITH CHICKEN BREAST

SERVES 4 ■

Preparation and cooking time: 30 minutes
Kcal per portion: 835
P = 67g, F = 22g, C = 92g

500g/1lb 2oz tagliatelle
salt
4 chicken breast fillets
50g/2oz butter
freshly ground black pepper
1 tsp herbes de Provence
250g/8oz frozen peas, thawed
3 eggs
250ml/9 fl oz milk
80g/3oz full-fat soft cheese with garlic

1. Cook the rigatoni in salted, boiling water until just al dente. Drain well in a sieve.
2. Cut the chicken breasts into strips. Reserving a little for the dish, heat the butter in a large frying pan. Add the chicken and fry briefly. Season with salt and pepper and sprinkle with the herbes de Provence.
3. Heat the oven to 200°C/400°F/Gas Mark 6. Butter a large ovenproof dish.
4. Mix the pasta with the peas and chicken strips and fill the dish.
5. Beat the eggs with the milk, mix with the garlic cheese and pour the mixture over the top of the dish.
6. Bake in the middle of the oven for 20 minutes until golden.
Side dish: mixed salad.
Recommended wine: a dry white.

ORIENTAL RICE BAKE

(photo page 92/93)

SERVES 4 ■
*Preparation and cooking
time: 30 minutes
Kcal per portion: 630
P = 41g, F = 23g, C = 66g*

500ml/16 fl oz chicken stock
250g/8oz quick-cook rice
500g/1lb 2oz turkey steaks
50g/2oz butter
120g/5oz mature Gouda
   cheese, grated
4 tbsps raisins
3 tbsps coarsely chopped
   almonds
salt
2 tbsps curry powder
pinch of cumin
freshly ground black pepper
400g/14oz can tomatoes

1. Bring the stock to the boil
and cook the rice in it for
about 5 minutes.
2. Cut the turkey into narrow
strips. Reserving a little for
the dish, heat half the butter
in a large frying pan. Add the
turkey and fry briefly.
3. Mix the rice with the fried
meat, half the cheese, the
raisins and the chopped
almonds. Season with salt,
pepper, curry powder and
cumin.
4. Heat the oven to
220°C/425°F/Gas Mark 7.
5. Drain the tomatoes in a
sieve, chop coarsely and mix
with the ingredients in the
pan.
6. Grease a soufflé dish with
the reserved butter. Fill the
dish with the rice mixture
and sprinkle the rest of the
grated cheese over the top.
7. Bake on the middle shelf
of the oven for 15–20 minutes until the cheese has
melted and turned golden
brown.
Side dish: cucumber salad
with yogurt.
Recommended drink: well-
chilled apple juice.

TORTELLINI AND VEGETABLES AU GRATIN

SERVES 4 ■
*Preparation and cooking
time: 30 minutes
Kcal per portion: 775
P = 36g, F = 24g, C = 104g*

500g/1lb 2oz ready-made
   spinach tortellini
salt
400g/14oz courgettes
45g/1½oz butter
2 garlic cloves
3 eggs
125ml/4 fl oz milk
100g/4oz grated Parmesan
   cheese
freshly ground black pepper
freshly grated nutmeg

1. Cook the tortellini according to the instructions, then
drain thoroughly in a sieve.
2. Wash the courgettes, cut
off their stalks and grate in a
food processor.
3. Heat the oven to
220°C/425°F/Gas Mark 7.
4. Heat about 30g/1oz butter in a pan and fry the grated courgettes over a high
heat for about 5 minutes,
stirring frequently. Crush the
garlic into the pan and season with salt.
5. Grease a dish with the
remaining butter. Spread the
courgettes over the bottom
of the dish, followed by a
layer of tortellini.
6. Beat the eggs and milk
together, mix with Parmesan
and season with salt, pepper
and nutmeg. Pour this mixture evenly over the dish.
7. Bake in the middle of the
oven for 15 minutes until the
surface turns a golden
brown.
Side dish: mixed green
salad.
Recommended wine: a light
Italian red.

*Wash the courgettes and grate in
a food processor.*

*Crush the peeled garlic into the
pan containing the courgettes.*

*Spread a layer of tortellini over
the vegetables.*

*Beat the eggs with milk and
grated Parmesan, then season
with salt, pepper and nutmeg.*

BAKED RICE WITH CHICKEN LIVERS

SERVES 4 ■
*Preparation and cooking
time: 25 minutes
Kcal per portion: 565
P = 39g, F = 22g, C = 52g*

500ml/16 fl oz chicken stock
250g/8oz quick-cook rice
500g/1lb 2oz chicken livers
60g/2oz butter
1 bunch spring onions
salt
freshly ground black pepper
1 tsp oregano
100g/4oz Gouda cheese

1. Bring the chicken stock to
the boil and cook the rice for
about 5 minutes. Set aside.
2. Chop the chicken livers
coarsely and fry briefly in
some butter. Set aside.
3. Wash and clean the spring
onions, cut them into fine
rings and sweat in the fat for
about 3 minutes.
4. Heat the oven to
200°C/400°F/Gas Mark 6.
5. Mix the rice with the
spring onions and chicken
livers and season well with
salt, pepper and oregano.
6. Grease a dish with butter
and fill with one-third of the
rice mixture, followed by a
layer of grated cheese.
Continue in this way and top
with a layer of cheese and
some flakes of butter.
7. Bake in the middle of the
oven for 10 minutes until
golden brown.
Side dish: tomato salad with
basil and vinaigrette dressing
or a mixed salad.
Recommended wine: a dry
red.

COD FILLET AU GRATIN

SERVES 4 ■
*Preparation and cooking
   time: 30 minutes
Kcal per portion: 270
P = 34g, F = 7g, C = 18g*

*3 rolls
2 eggs
125ml/4 fl oz milk
1 bunch of parsley
3 garlic cloves
salt
freshly ground black pepper
1 tbsp olive oil
4 x 150g/5½oz cod fillets
lemon juice
3 tbsps capers*

1. Cut the rolls into thin slices.
2. Beat together the eggs and milk. Finely chop the parsley, crush the garlic and add it to the egg mixture. Season well with salt and pepper.

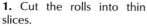

> **TIP**
>
> *The fish can also be laid on a bed of sliced tomato or spinach.*

3. Heat the oven to 220°C/425°F/Gas Mark 7.
4. Wash the fish, pat it dry, sprinkle with lemon juice and season with salt and pepper.
5. Brush an ovenproof dish with olive oil and lay the fish in it; scatter capers over the top.
6. Cover the fish with overlapping layers of bread and pour the egg mixture over the top.
7. Bake in the middle of the oven for 15–20 minutes until golden.
Side dish: tomato salad.
Recommended wine: a light red, e.g. Beaujolais Villages.

Slice the rolls thinly.

Add the finely chopped parsley to the beaten eggs and milk.

Wash the fish and pat it dry; sprinkle with lemon juice, salt and pepper.

Lay the fish in an ovenproof dish and top with overlapping layers of bread.

BAKED SAUERKRAUT AND LIVER SAUSAGE

SERVES 4 ■
*Preparation and cooking
   time: 30 minutes
Kcal per portion: 450
P = 25g, F = 29g, C = 22g*

*4 portions instant mashed
   potato
butter for the dish
two 450g/1lb jars sauerkraut
300g/10oz liver sausage
100g/4oz Emmental cheese,
   grated
salt
freshly ground black pepper*

1. Prepare the mashed potato using milk or water, according to instructions.
2. Heat the oven to 220°C/425°F/Gas Mark 7.
3. Butter an ovenproof dish and spread half the potato over the bottom, followed by half the sauerkraut.
4. Remove the skin and spread the liver sausage over the sauerkraut.
5. Mix the remaining potato with half the cheese and use this mixture as a topping. Smooth the surface, then sprinkle with the remaining cheese and a little salt and pepper.
6. Bake in the middle of the oven for 20 minutes until golden.
This dish also tastes good made with leftover roast or minced meat instead of liver sausage.
Recommended drinks: beer or a dry Riesling.

BAKED LEEKS WITH GARLIC SAUSAGE

SERVES 4 ■
*Preparation and cooking
   time: 35 minutes
Kcal per portion: 575
P = 34g, F = 44g, C = 11g*

*750g/1lb10oz leeks
salt
400g/14oz garlic sausage
butter for the dish
375ml/15 fl oz milk
4 eggs
freshly ground black pepper
80g/3oz grated Parmesan
   cheese*

1. Trim the leeks, slit them open lengthways and wash thoroughly. Cut into small rings and blanch for 1 minute in salted, boiling water. Rinse in a sieve under cold water and drain.

> **TIP**
>
> *Vary this dish by using other types of cooked sausage, boiled ham or hot-smoked fish such as mackerel.*

2. Remove the sausage skin and, if it is in a piece, cut it into thin slices.
3. Heat the oven to 220°C/425°F/Gas Mark 7.
4. Butter a large ovenproof dish. Fill with alternate layers of leeks and sausage, finishing with leeks.
5. Beat together the milk and eggs. Season with salt and pepper, add the Parmesan and pour over the leeks and sausage.
6. Bake in the middle of the oven for 20 minutes.
Side dish: crusty bread.
Recommended drink: cider.

FENNEL AND CHEESE AU GRATIN

SERVES 4
*Preparation and cooking
   time: 30 minutes*
Kcal per portion: 525
P = 21g, F = 41g, C = 14g

*1kg/2¼lbs fennel
salt
butter for the dish
20ml/1 tbsp Pernod
   (optional)
200ml/6 fl oz crème fraîche
100g/4oz Gouda cheese
150g/5½oz Roquefort or
   Stilton cheese
freshly ground black pepper*

*Cut off the fennel tops and slice
the bulbs thinly lengthways.*

1. Remove the fennel tops (reserve some for garnishing), wash the bulbs and cut them into thin slices lengthways. Cook the slices for 3–4 minutes in salted, boiling water. Drain in a sieve.

TIP

*This dish can
also be made
with kohlrabi,
and may be
enriched by
adding some
strips of fried
turkey breast.*

*If liked, sprinkle the blanched
fennel with Pernod to enhance
the aniseed flavour.*

*Mix the crème fraîche with grated
Gouda, then crumble in the
Roquefort or Stilton.*

2. Heat the oven to 200°C/400°F/Gas Mark 6.
3. Put the fennel slices in a buttered dish. Pour on an even sprinkling of Pernod, if using.
4. Grate the Gouda and combine it with the crème fraîche. Crumble in the Stilton; season with pepper.
5. Spread an even layer of the cheese mixture over the fennel. Bake in the middle of the oven for 15 minutes until golden. Sprinkle with chopped fennel tops.
Side dish: mixed salad.
Recommended drink: pilsner beer.

*Spread an even layer of cheese
mixture over the fennel.*

SPINACH AND MOZZARELLA AU GRATIN

SERVES 4
*Preparation and cooking
   time: 30 minutes*
Kcal per portion: 360
P = 26g, F = 26g, C = 3g

*750g/1lb 10oz frozen spinach,
   thawed
1 onion, finely chopped
30g/1oz butter
salt
freshly ground black pepper
freshly grated nutmeg
4 eggs
2 Mozzarella cheeses,
   150g/5½oz each*

1. Squeeze some of the moisture out of the spinach, then fry it with the onion in some butter for about 10 minutes. Season with salt, pepper and nutmeg then allow to cool.
2. Beat the eggs and mix them into the lukewarm spinach.
3. Heat the oven to 200°C/400°F/Gas Mark 6.
4. Fill a buttered dish with the spinach and egg mixture.
5. Cut the Mozzarella into slices and arrange the slices in overlapping layers on top of the spinach. Season with salt and pepper.
6. Bake in the middle of the oven for 20 minutes until the cheese has melted and the eggs have thickened. Serve hot from the oven.
About 250g/8oz mortadella can be mixed with the spinach.
Side dish: potato purée.
Recommended wine: a dry white.

POACHED EGGS ON A SPINACH BED

SERVES 4
*Preparation and cooking
   time: 25 minutes*
Kcal per portion: 490
P = 26g, F = 41g, C = 4g

*1 onion
100g/4oz Gruyère cheese
30g/1oz butter
600g/1lb 6oz frozen spinach,
   thawed
salt
freshly ground white pepper
freshly grated nutmeg
8 tbsps vinegar
8 eggs
200ml/6 fl oz single cream*

1. Dice the onion finely. Grate the cheese.
2. Reserving a little for the dish, heat the butter in a pan and fry the onion until transparent. Add the spinach and cook gently for 5 minutes. Season well with salt, pepper and nutmeg.
3. Heat the oven to 200°C/400°F/Gas Mark 6.
4. Bring 2l/3½ pints of water to the boil and add the vinegar. Break the eggs into a cup and slip them into the barely simmering water. Cook the eggs for 3 minutes, then lift them out with a slotted spoon and set aside to drain well. (You may find it easier to cook the eggs in two batches.)
5. Grease a large ovenproof dish with the reserved butter. Put the spinach in a buttered dish. Make eight hollows in the surface with a spoon and place the eggs on top.
6. Combine the cream and cheese and pour it over the eggs. Bake in the middle of the oven for 10 minutes.
Side dish: mashed or sautéed potatoes and mixed green salad.
Recommended wine: a dry white.

Microwave Recipes

106

*D*elicate egg dishes are perfect for the standard microwave. It cooks Pearl Barley Mould to a perfect consistency. For grilled dishes a combination grill or hot air and microwave oven is needed to achieve that crispy top layer.

Savings in cooking time become plain when one realises that Potatoes au Gratin will take only 16–18 minutes in a combination microwave, against about 50 minutes in a conventional oven. The lack of a combination oven does not entirely prevent the preparation of baked egg dishes. Tuna and Pepper Tortilla or a hearty Creamy Bread and Cheese Bake will simply turn out juicy instead of browned and crispy.

Potatoes au Gratin
(recipe page 113)

BAKED RICE AND FRANKFURTERS

SERVES 4 ■■
Combination microwave
Preparation and cooking
time: 1 hour
Kcal per portion: 660
P = 27g, F = 41g, C = 46g

1 red and 1 yellow pepper
5 spring onions
2 garlic cloves
4 Frankfurter sausages
4 tbsps oil
200g/7oz long-grain rice
250ml/8 fl oz beef stock
400g/14oz can tomatoes
salt
freshly ground black pepper
1 tsp paprika
1 small piece of dried chilli, chopped
½ tsp dried marjoram
4 eggs
50g/2oz Cheddar cheese, grated
2 tbsps chopped fresh parsley

1. Halve the peppers and remove the seeds and pith. Remove the roots and part of the green tops from the onions. Peel the garlic. Dice these vegetables finely.
2. Cut the sausages into rings and put them in a microwave dish with the vegetables. Sprinkle with the oil and cook for *4–5 minutes at 600 watts*.
3. Stir in the rice and pour on the stock; chop the tomatoes, add with their juice and season with salt, pepper, paprika and chilli. Cover and cook for *5 minutes at 600 watts*, then *20–22 minutes at 180 watts*.
4. Turn on the grill.
5. Beat the eggs with 40g/1½oz of cheese and the parsley and mix into the baked rice. Smooth the surface, sprinkle with the remaining cheese and cook for *6–8 minutes at 180 watts* with the grill on.
Side dish: chicory salad.
Recommended drink: beer.

PEARL BARLEY MOULD

SERVES 2 ■■
Standard microwave
Preparation and cooking
time: 40 minutes
Kcal per portion: 615
P = 29g, F = 37g, C = 40g

250ml/8 fl oz vegetable stock
100g/4oz pearl barley
sprig of thyme
1 carrot
1 small leek
1 garlic clove
30g/1oz butter
50g/2oz frozen peas, thawed
2 tbsps chopped herbs (parsley, chervil, basil)
2 tbsps chopped pistachio nuts
75g/3oz Cheddar cheese, grated
1 tbsp crème fraîche
2 eggs, separated
salt
freshly ground black pepper
½ tsp curry powder

1. Bring the stock to the boil in a microwave dish. Add the pearl barley and thyme, cover and cook for *5 minutes at 360 watts* and *5 minutes at 180 watts*.

> ### TIP
> *This mould is sufficient as a side dish for 4 people. The vegetable selection can be varied to suit all tastes.*

2. Meanwhile, wash the carrot and leek thoroughly and cut them into small cubes. Chop the garlic finely. Put the garlic in a large microwave dish with the diced carrot and leek and dot with most of the butter.
3. Take the barley out of the oven, cover the dish and set aside to continue swelling. Remove the thyme sprig. Put the dish of vegetables in the

Stir the pearl barley into the hot vegetable stock. Add the thyme and cook for 10 minutes, then leave to soak.

Mix the barley with the vegetables, herbs, pistachio nuts, cheese, crème fraîche and egg yolks.

oven, cover and cook for *4–5 minutes at 600 watts*.
4. Add the barley to the vegetables, along with the peas, herbs, pistachios, cheese, crème fraîche and egg yolks. Season with salt, pepper and curry powder. Whisk the egg whites until they stand in stiff peaks and fold them in.
5. Butter a 1l/1¾-pint microwave pudding basin. Put in the vegetable mixture, cover and cook for *7–8 minutes at 600 watts*.
6. Leave covered and stand for about 5 minutes after cooking, then turn out onto a plate.
Side dish: tomato sauce and a mixed salad.
Recommended wine: a dry, spicy white.

GREEN NOODLE BAKE

SERVES 4 ■■
Combination microwave
Preparation and cooking
time: 1 hour
Kcal per portion: 800
P = 40g, F = 55g, C = 36g

200g/7oz green tagliatelle
salt
200g/7oz lean raw ham
300g/10oz spinach purée
200ml/6 fl oz crème fraîche
50g/2oz grated Parmesan cheese
100g/4oz Cheddar cheese, grated
5 eggs, beaten
salt
freshly ground black pepper
freshly grated nutmeg
40g/1½oz butter

1. Boil the tagliatelle for about 5 minutes in plenty of salted, boiling water. Drain well.
2. Heat the combination oven to 180°C/350°F.
3. Cut the ham into small cubes and mix thoroughly with the spinach, crème fraîche, Parmesan, half the Cheddar and the eggs. Season with salt, pepper and nutmeg.
4. Mix the tagliatelle with the spinach mixture.
5. Butter a large microwave dish. Top with the remaining cheese and dot with butter.
6. Bake on the middle shelf for *18–20 minutes at 360 watts and 180°C/350°F (hot air 160°C/310°F)*. Stand for a while before serving.
Side dish: green salad.
Recommended wine: a light Italian red.

BAKED MEATBALLS

SERVES 4 ■
Combination microwave
Preparation and cooking
time: 40 minutes
Kcal per portion: 640
P = 37g, F = 52g, C = 5g

1 onion
1 garlic clove
½ bunch parsley
500g/1lb 2oz minced steak
1 tbsp flour
4 eggs
1 tsp Dijon mustard
salt
freshly ground black pepper
40g/1½oz butter or margarine
250ml/9 fl oz soured cream
½ tsp paprika
½ tsp dried marjoram

1. Dice the onion and garlic. Wash and dry the parsley and chop finely. Put all three in a bowl and add the meat, flour and 1 egg. Season with salt, pepper and mustard and knead to a smooth dough.

Form the meat mixture into balls 4cm/1½ inches in diameter.

Pour the beaten eggs and cream over the meatballs.

> ### TIP
> *Complete the meal by placing a layer of sliced boiled potatoes in the dish as a bed for the meatballs.*

2. Heat the combination oven to 200°C/400°F.
3. Grease a microwave dish with some of the fat. Make 4 cm/1½-inch diameter balls out of the meat mixture and arrange them in a circle in the dish.
4. Leave uncovered and cook for *4–5 minutes at 600 watts and 200°C/400°F (hot air 180°C/350°F)*.
5. Beat the soured cream with the remaining eggs, then season with salt, pepper, paprika and marjoram.

6. Pour the mixture evenly over the meatballs and dot with butter or margarine. Brown for *6–8 minutes at 600 watts* with the grill switched on.
Side dish: fried potatoes and chicory salad.
Recommended drink: pilsner beer.

CREAMY BREAD AND CHEESE BAKE

SERVES 2 ■
Standard microwave
Preparation and cooking
time: 30 minutes
Kcal per portion: 965
P = 34g, F = 81g, C = 26g

100g/4oz stale wholemeal bread
50g/2oz Cheddar cheese, grated
50g/2oz grated Parmesan cheese
250ml/8 fl oz single cream
3 eggs
1 tsp tomato purée
1 garlic clove, finely chopped
1 tsp fresh thyme leaves
1 tbsp chopped fresh parsley
salt
freshly ground black pepper
40g/1½oz butter
½ tsp paprika

1. Use a food processor to turn the bread into fine crumbs. Mix with both types of cheese and put in a bowl.
2. Beat the cream with the eggs, tomato purée, garlic and herbs, then season with salt and pepper.
3. Grease a microwave dish with a little of the butter. Put the breadcrumbs and cheese mixture in the dish. Cover with the beaten eggs and cream and leave to stand for 10 minutes.
4. Dot with the remaining butter and dust with paprika. Cook uncovered for *7–9 minutes at 600 watts*.
If the bread is too moist to begin with, put it in the microwave on full power for about 2 minutes.
Side dish: tomato sauce and mixed salad.

TUNA AND PEPPER TORTILLA

SERVES 2 ■ ■
Standard microwave
Preparation and cooking
time: 40 minutes
Kcal per portion: 345
P = 11g, F = 20g, C = 30g

400g/14oz waxy potatoes
1 onion
1 red pepper
4 tbsps olive oil
4 eggs
1 tbsp chopped fresh parsley
salt
freshly ground white pepper
100g/4oz canned tuna

1. Peel the potatoes and slice them wafer thin.
2. Wash and halve the red pepper, then remove the seeds, pith and stalk. Dice the pepper and the onion and mix them with the potatoes.
3. Put the vegetables in a round microwave dish. Sprinkle with the oil, cover and precook for *8–10 minutes at 600 watts*.
4. Beat the eggs thoroughly with the parsley and season with salt and pepper.
5. Drain the tuna, break it into pieces and mix with the precooked vegetables. Pour the beaten eggs over the mixture and cook for *4 minutes at 600 watts*. Stir once during cooking to ensure that the eggs thicken evenly.
6. Let the tortilla stand for a few minutes before serving, either turned out on a plate or straight from the dish.
Side dish: mixed salad.
Recommended wine: a light rosé.

KOHLRABI AU GRATIN
WITH PISTACHIO NUTS

KOHLRABI AU GRATIN WITH PISTACHIO NUTS

SERVES 2 ■
Combination microwave
Preparation and cooking
time: 30 minutes
Kcal per portion: 580
P = 15g, F = 53g, C = 10g

2 young kohlrabi (200g/7oz
each)
1 small onion
50g/2oz bacon
2 tbsps oil
150ml/5½ fl oz crème fraîche
2 tbsps grated Parmesan
cheese
1 tbsp chopped fresh parsley
salt
freshly ground white pepper
butter for the dish
2 tbsps chopped pistachio
nuts

1. Trim off the kohlrabi leaves. Shred the tender inner ones finely and set them aside. Peel the root and cut it into thin slices crossways. Dice the onion and bacon.

> ### TIP
> *A similar dish*
> *can be prepared*
> *using carrots*
> *instead of*
> *kohlrabi.*

2. Heat the combination oven to 200°C/400°F.
3. Put the diced bacon and onion into a microwave dish with the oil and cook for *3–4 minutes at 600 watts*, until they turn transparent.
4. Combine the crème fraîche, Parmesan, parsley and shredded kohlrabi leaves with the bacon and onion and season well with salt and pepper.
5. Butter a circular microwave dish. Arrange a layer of kohlrabi in it, followed by some of the crème fraîche mixture. Cover this

Cut the kohlrabi into thin slices, preferably with a mandolin.

Mix together the crème fraîche, Parmesan, onions, bacon, parsley and kohlrabi leaves.

Arrange alternate layers of the cream mixture and kohlrabi slices in a dish.

with more kohlrabi and continue layering until all the ingredients are used up. Use crème fraîche as a topping.
6. Sprinkle the dish with pistachio nuts and cook on the middle shelf of the oven for *14–16 minutes at 600 watts and 200°C/400°F (hot air 180°C/350°F).*
Serve as an accompaniment to veal or pork fillets.

FENNEL AND APPLES AU GRATIN

SERVES 4 ■
Combination microwave
Preparation and cooking
time: 35 minutes
Kcal per portion: 420
P = 3g, F = 37g, C = 18g

2 fennel bulbs (300g/10oz
each)
4 apples (Cox's)
50g/2oz butter
juice of 1 lemon
200ml/6 fl oz single cream
100ml/3 fl oz crème fraîche
salt
freshly ground white pepper
freshly grated nutmeg

1. Wash and peel the fennel, then cut it into thin slices. (Reserve some of the leaves to use as a topping if liked.) Peel and core the apples, then cut them into slices 5 mm/¼ inch thick.
2. Heat the combination oven to 220°C/425°F.
3. Grease an oval microwave dish with a little of the butter. Arrange alternate layers of fennel and apple slices in it and sprinkle with lemon juice.
4. Beat together the eggs, cream and crème fraîche and season with salt, pepper and nutmeg. Pour over the fennel and apple. Dot with the remaining butter and sprinkle with shredded fennel tops if using.
5. Leave the dish uncovered and bake for *13–15 minutes at 600 watts and 220°C/ 425°F (hot air 200°C/ 400°F).*
Serve as an accompaniment to game.

POTATOES AU GRATIN

(photo page 106/107)

SERVES 4 ■
Combination microwave
Preparation time: 30 minutes
Kcal per portion: 555
P = 13g, F = 41g, C = 34g

800g/1lb 12oz floury potatoes
2 garlic cloves
40g/1½oz butter
salt
freshly ground white pepper
freshly grated nutmeg
100g/4oz Cheddar cheese,
grated
250ml/9 fl oz single cream

1. Heat the combination oven to 250°C/475°F.
2. Peel the potatoes and cut them into thin slices.
3. Crush the garlic cloves and combine them with the butter. Grease a microwave pie dish with half this garlic butter.
4. Arrange a layer of sliced potato in the dish and season with salt, pepper and nutmeg; also add a sprinkling of cheese. Arrange another layer of potatoes and continue until all the ingredients are used up, finishing with potato slices.
5. Pour the cream over the dish and dot with the remaining butter.
6. Leave uncovered and bake for *16–18 minutes at 600 watts and 250°C/475°F (hot air 220°C/425°F)* until golden brown.
Serve as an accompaniment to steak or grilled lamb, or as a main dish for two people with a side dish of mixed salad.

COURGETTES AND AUBERGINES AU GRATIN

SERVES 4 ■
Combination microwave
Preparation and cooking
*   time: 35 minutes*
Kcal per portion: 200
P = 5g, F = 17g, C = 6g

2 small courgettes
1 small aubergine
4 beefsteak tomatoes
1 onion
1–2 garlic cloves
6 tbsps olive oil
salt
freshly ground white pepper
1 tsp fresh thyme leaves
30g/1oz grated Parmesan
   cheese

Wash the courgettes and aubergines and trim off both ends.

1. Wash the courgettes and aubergines, remove the stalks, then slice the vegetables thinly.

Arrange an overlapping layer of sliced vegetables on the layer of tomatoes.

> **TIP**
> *Sliced potatoes can also be layered between the courgettes and aubergines. To speed up preparation, use canned chopped tomatoes.*

2. Wash the tomatoes, cut a cross in their skins near the stalk and place in the microwave for *2–3 minutes at 600 watts*. Plunge them into cold water, peel and cut into chunks, discarding the seeds and stalks.
3. Chop the onion and garlic finely. Put them into an oval microwave dish, sprinkle with three tablespoons of the oil and cook for *3–4 minutes at 600 watts* until they turn transparent.
4. Add the tomatoes and season with salt and pepper.

Leave uncovered and cook for *4 minutes at 600 watts*.
5. Heat the combination oven to 220°C/425°F.
6. Take out half the tomatoes and set them aside. Spread the rest out in an even layer on the bottom of the dish. Arrange alternate rows of courgette and aubergine slices, slightly overlapping. Cover with the reserved tomatoes and sprinkle with thyme and Parmesan. Sprinkle the remaining olive oil over the top.
7. Bake on the middle shelf of the oven for *16–18 minutes at 600 watts and 220°C/425°F (hot air 200°C/400°F)* until golden brown.
Recommended wine: a strong red if served with meat.

TOMATOES AU GRATIN

SERVES 4 ■
Combination microwave
Preparation and cooking
*   time: 20 minutes*
Kcal per portion: 95
P = 2g, F = 8g, C = 3g

4 ripe tomatoes
salt
1 shallot
1–2 garlic cloves
3 tbsps olive oil
½ tsp herbes de Provence
1 tbsp chopped parsley
1 tbsp breadcrumbs
1 tbsp grated Parmesan
   cheese

1. Wash the tomatoes and cut them in half crossways. Sprinkle the cut surfaces with salt and lay them with this face down on a plate to drain.
2. Heat the grill in the combination oven.

> **TIP**
> *The paste spreads best if fresh breadcrumbs and sun-ripened tomatoes are used.*

3. Chop the shallot and garlic finely. Put them in a microwave dish and cook them for 2 minutes at 600 watts.
4. Add the herbes de Provence, parsley, breadcrumbs and Parmesan and mix everything to a paste.
5. Spread the cut surfaces of the tomatoes with shallot paste. Arrange the tomato halves in a circle on an ovenproof microwave dish.
6. Bake on the top shelf of the oven for *2–3 minutes at 600 watts* with the grill switched on.
Serve as an accompaniment to steak or lamb chops.

To ensure that the tomatoes cook evenly and look attractive, select ones of equal size.

Wash the tomatoes, cut them in half and sprinkle with salt.

Spread the shallot paste over the tomatoes and arrange the tomatoes in a circle on a plate.

Lean Cuisine

*E*gg dishes need not be calorie bombs; fat and cream can be used sparingly in conjunction with more luxurious vegetables and herbs. Egg dishes like Italian-style Omelette or Omelette with Snails form an appropriate element of diet cooking if one knows when to use ingredients sparingly and when to allow a little leniency.

There is absolutely no need for the slim-minded gourmet to starve when there are dishes like Mushrooms and Tomatoes au Gratin or Potato and Prawn Bake. In these recipes the attraction lies more in the flavour than in the quantity.

Omelette with Snails
(recipe page 118)

SPINACH-FILLED CHEESE OMELETTE

SERVES 2   ■■
*Preparation and cooking
    time: 25 minutes
Kcal per portion: 325
P = 22g, F = 25g, C = 3g*

300g/10oz young spinach
1 garlic clove
1 onion
15g/½oz butter
salt
freshly ground white pepper
freshly grated nutmeg
4 eggs
1 tbsp water
2 tbsps grated Parmesan
    cheese
2 tsps oil

1. Pick over and wash the spinach, then drain in a sieve. Chop the onion and garlic finely.

> **TIP**
>
> *Instead of
> spinach, try
> chard or sorrel
> leaves as a filling.*

2. Heat the butter and fry the onion and garlic. Add the spinach, season with salt, pepper and nutmeg, cover and cook over a medium heat.
3. Meanwhile beat the eggs, water and cheese together with salt and pepper to taste.
4. Take two small non-stick frying pans and heat a teaspoon of oil in each. Divide the beaten egg between them and cook over a medium heat.
5. Slip the omelettes onto heated plates, top with spinach and fold in half.
Side dish: boiled new potatoes.

OMELETTE WITH SNAILS

(photo page 116/117)

SERVES 2   ■
*Preparation and cooking
    time: 20 minutes
Kcal per portion: 315
P = 23g, F = 24g, C = 1g*

12 canned snails
2 garlic cloves
1 shallot
4 eggs
1 tbsp water
salt
freshly ground black pepper
2 tbsps oil
1 tbsp chopped fresh parsley

1. Chop the snails coarsely, using a sharp knife. Dice the garlic and shallot very fine.
2. Beat the eggs thoroughly with the water, salt and pepper.
3. Take two 20cm/8-inch non-stick pans and heat a tablespoon of oil in each. Gently fry half the chopped garlic, shallots and escargots in each pan.
4. Pour in the beaten egg and cook over a medium heat.
5. Fold up the omelettes and slip each onto a heated plate.
The omelettes can also be prepared separately from the escargots and then filled.
Side dish: crusty white bread.

*Chop the snails coarsely with a
sharp knife.*

*Cook the garlic, shallot and snails
gently in oil.*

*Pour the seasoned beaten egg
over the snails and cook.*

Fold up the omelettes and serve.

ITALIAN-STYLE OMELETTE

SERVES 2   ■
*Preparation and cooking
    time: 20 minutes
Kcal per portion: 285
P = 15g, F = 23g, C = 4g*

2 garlic cloves
2 beefsteak tomatoes
4 eggs
1 tbsp water
salt
freshly ground black pepper
2 tbsps olive oil
6–8 chopped basil leaves

1. Chop the garlic very finely. Blanch and skin the tomatoes. Remove the stalk and seeds and chop the flesh into small cubes.
2. Beat the eggs, water, salt and pepper thoroughly with a fork.

> **TIP**
>
> *Use only a fork to
> beat the eggs, not
> a wire whisk. The
> result should not
> be too foamy or
> the omelette will
> not have a
> creamy
> consistency.*

3. Take two 20cm/8-inch non-stick pans and heat a tablespoon of oil in each. Sweat half the chopped garlic and tomatoes in each.
4. Sprinkle with basil leaves and pour in the beaten egg. Cook over a medium heat.
5. Fold up the omelettes and serve them on heated plates.
Side dish: toasted white bread.

MUSHROOMS AND TOMATOES AU GRATIN

SERVES 2
*Preparation and cooking
time: 50 minutes
Kcal per portion: 165
P = 7g, F = 12g, C = 8g*

1 large onion
2 garlic cloves
250g/8oz shiitake or button
mushrooms
30g/1oz butter
salt
freshly ground black pepper
2 large beefsteak tomatoes
1 tsp oil
½ tsp fresh thyme leaves
1 tbsp chopped fresh parsley
1 tbsp breadcrumbs
1 tbsp grated Parmesan
cheese

1. Heat the oven to 220°C/425°F/Gas Mark 7.
2. Chop the onion and garlic finely. Wipe the mushrooms; halve or quarter larger specimens.
3. Heat the butter in a non-stick pan and fry the onion and garlic gently. Add the mushrooms and cook together briefly. Season with salt and pepper and remove from the heat.
4. Blanch, peel and slice the tomatoes.
5. Brush one large oval oven-proof dish or two individual dishes with oil. Fill with alternate layers of sliced tomatoes and mushrooms, sprinkling thyme and parsley between each layer. Mix the Parmesan and breadcrumbs and sprinkle evenly over the top of the dish.
6. Bake for about 15 minutes in the top of the oven.
Side dish: baked potatoes with soured cream, or serve as an accompaniment to lamb chops.

Gently fry the onions and garlic in oil, then add the mushrooms.

Peel and slice the tomatoes.

Arrange layers of tomatoes and mushrooms in a dish.

Top with a sprinkling of Parmesan and breadcrumbs.

POTATO AND PRAWN BAKE

(photo page 21)

SERVES 4
*Preparation and cooking
time: 50 minutes
Kcal per portion: 275
P = 20g, F = 10g, C = 27g*

600g/1lb 12oz potatoes boiled
in their skins
150g/5½oz frozen peas
200g/7oz peeled prawns
3 egg yolks
100ml/3 fl oz soured cream
salt
freshly ground white pepper
1 tbsp chopped fresh dill
3 egg whites
butter for the dish

1. Heat the oven to 200°C/400°F/Gas Mark 6.

TIP
Instead of prawns, diced bacon may be used.

2. Peel the potatoes and grate them coarsely. Add the peas and prawns and gradually mix in the egg yolks and soured cream, stirring all the time. Season with salt, pepper and dill.
3. Beat the egg whites until they stand in stiff peaks and gently fold them into the potato mixture. Butter an 18cm/7-inch ovenproof dish.
4. Bake in the middle of the oven for 25–30 minutes until golden brown.
Side dish: cucumber salad.

Grate the potatoes coarsely.

Combine the peas, prawns and potatoes with the egg yolks.

Stir the soured cream into the vegetable and prawn mixture.

Whisk the egg whites and fold them into the mixture.

CARROTS AND LEEKS AU GRATIN

SERVES 4 ■
Preparation and cooking time: 1 hour
Kcal per portion: 210
P = 7g, F = 16g, C = 10g

500g/1lb 2oz carrots
2 large leeks (400g/14oz when trimmed)
10g/¼oz butter for the dish
100ml/3 fl oz soured cream
100ml/3 fl oz single cream
40g/1½oz grated cheese
salt
freshly ground white pepper
freshly grated nutmeg

1. Heat the oven to 200°C/400°F/Gas Mark 6.
2. Peel the carrots and slice thinly, preferably with a vegetable slicer or in a food processor. Trim off the root and green ends of the leeks. Cut the white part into thin rings, wash thoroughly in cold water and drain.

TIP

Instead of carrots, potatoes also make a harmonious accompaniment to leeks.

---

3. Butter a round ovenproof dish and arrange a ring of sliced carrots, followed by a ring of leek slices. Continue with alternating rings and layers of vegetables until they are all used up.
4. Mix together the two types of cream, add the cheese and combine thoroughly. Season with salt, pepper and nutmeg. Pour evenly over the vegetables.
5. Bake for about 45 minutes in the middle of the oven. Serve as an accompaniment to meat, or with potatoes as a meal for two.

Emmental or farmhouse Cheddar are particularly good cheeses for dishes au gratin.

Peel the carrots and use a slicer to cut them into thin rings.

Arrange rings of carrot and leek in layers in a round dish.

CHICORY AND MOZZARELLA AU GRATIN

SERVES 2 ■
Preparation and cooking time: 40 minutes
Kcal per portion: 205
P = 14g, F = 13g, C = 7g

4 chicory heads (150g/5½oz each)
salt
2 beefsteak tomatoes
½ bunch of basil
100g/4oz Mozzarella cheese
10g/¼oz butter for the dish
freshly ground black pepper

1. Clean the chicory and with a sharp knife, cut a cone out of the bitter root end. Cook for about 8 minutes in salted, boiling water.
2. Heat the oven to 220°C/425°F/Gas Mark 7.
3. Blanch and peel the tomatoes. Remove the stalk and seeds and chop the flesh into small cubes. Wash and dry the basil, then cut it into strips. Cut the Mozzarella into small cubes.
4. Lift the chicory out with a slotted spoon and drain well. Butter an ovenproof dish and arrange the chicory in it. Sprinkle with the tomatoes, basil and cheese and season with pepper.
5. Bake in the top of the oven for 10–15 minutes until golden brown.
This dish can be made more filling by wrapping the chicory in slices of ham before baking.
Side dish: boiled new potatoes.

STUFFED JACKET POTATOES

SERVES 4 ■
Preparation and cooking time: 1 hour
Kcal per portion: 200
P = 7g, F = 6g, C = 27

four 200g/7oz floury potatoes
1 fully ripe pear
a little lemon juice
75g/3oz Roquefort or Stilton cheese
1 tbsp vodka (optional)
salt
freshly ground black pepper

1. Heat the oven to 220°C/425°F/Gas Mark 7.
2. Scrub the potatoes thoroughly and dry them well on absorbent paper. Place them on a wire rack and bake in the middle of the oven for about 40 minutes.
3. Peel and halve the pear, remove the seeds and cut it into small cubes. Sprinkle with lemon juice.
4. Make a cross-shaped cut in each potato. Peel the skin back a little and carefully scoop out the flesh with a spoon, leaving a small amount adhering to the skin.
5. Mash the potato with a fork, or purée it with a hand-held mixer. Gradually add the cheese. Finally add the diced pear and season with salt, pepper and the vodka if using.
6. Stuff the potato skins with this mixture and arrange them on an ovenproof dish.
7. Bake in the top of the oven for 5–7 minutes.
Side dish: cranberries.

Index